THE SUPREME COURT

AND THE IDEA

OF PROGRESS

Alexander M. Bickel

THE SUPREME COURT
AND THE IDEA
OF PROGRESS

Foreword by Anthony Lewis

New Haven and London, Yale University Press
1978

This book is for my mother

Library of Congress catalog card number: 77–18365
International standard book number: 0–300–02238–7 (cloth)
0–300–02239–5 (paper)

The first edition of *The Supreme Court and the Idea of
Progress* was published by Harper & Row, Publishers, Inc.,
in 1970.

Printed in the United States of America by
LithoCrafters, Inc., Chelsea, Michigan.

Published in Great Britain, Europe, Africa, and Asia
(except Japan) by Yale University Press, Ltd., London.
Distributed in Latin America by Kaiman & Polon, Inc.,
New York City; in Australia and New Zealand by
Book & Film Services, Artarmon, N.S.W., Australia; and
in Japan by Harper & Row, Publishers, Tokyo Office.

Acknowledgment is made for use of the following material:

The excerpt on page 173 from "In Memory of Sigmund
Freud (d. September 1939)" is taken from *Collected
Shorter Poems, 1927–1957* by W. H. Auden. Copyright
1940 and renewed 1968 by W. H. Auden. Reprinted by
permission of Random House, Inc.

The excerpt on page 11 from "Thoughts Without Words"
is taken from *The Best of Clarence Day*, copyright 1948 by
Katherine B. Day. Reprinted by permission of Alfred A.
Knopf, Inc.

Contents

Foreword

We live in a democracy and celebrate our belief in self-government. But we give the last word to nine judges, appointed with life tenure, responsible to no electorate; we let them define premises as fundamental as the country's voting processes, its race relations, its sexual morality. That is the great paradox of the American system. In every generation it is savored anew, forced upon the national consciousness by conflict between the Supreme Court and some great popular feeling: John Marshall building Federal supremacy against the Jeffersonian belief in localism, Roger B. Taney arousing Abolitionist sentiment with the Dred Scott Case, Earl Warren outraging Southern and conservative opinion on issues of race and communism and the criminal law.

The paradox of judge-made law as the ultimate authority in a democracy was the subject that engaged Alexander M. Bickel in his intense, productive, too-short life as a critical student of the Supreme Court. He was in a great tradition of scholarly critics, going back to James Bradley Thayer and Felix Frankfurter. Like them he served the particular American function of subjecting the judicial power to the restraints of reason—of skeptical analysis, of philosophical inquiry. In the absence of direct political control, reasoned criticism has had its effect on judicial ideas. If American judges are the most powerful on earth, so too American law schools and legal writers are the most influential.

Professor Bickel was in the tradition of those who have doubted the perfect wisdom of judges, but his situation differed in one vital respect from that of the great critics in the earlier years of this century. Their target was a Supreme Court that read into the Constitution such conservative notions as "liberty of contract" and struck down reformist legislation on child labor, union rights and the like. The critics tended, therefore, to have the sympathy of the liberal, enlightened elements in the community, often the most articulate. But Professor Bickel criticized a Supreme Court that took enlightened positions on issues of race and civil liberties—undoubtedly the most "liberal" Court in our history. And so, inevitably, he puzzled or provoked much of his natural audience.

The Supreme Court and the Idea of Progress had

just such an effect at birth, in the lectures from which
Alex Bickel drew the book: the Oliver Wendell Holmes
Lectures at the Harvard Law School in October, 1969. I
heard the lectures and wrote about them in a column
for *The New York Times* that may be worth quoting for
a contemporaneous impression of Professor Bickel's
impact:

> Like other professional scrutineers of the Warren
> Court, he found much wrong with particular opin-
> ions: bad history, sloppy analysis. But there have al-
> ways been those faults, he said, and the modern
> Court is not going to be faulted by history on details
> if in fact it was "seized of a great vision," if it
> "glimpsed the future and gained it."
>
> But it was there that Professor Bickel parted com-
> pany with the liberal admirers of the Warren Court.
> To the evident shock of his audience, he argued that
> on the two greatest issues with which it had dealt—
> schools and voting—the Court misread the American
> future. He could not have put it more boldly than
> he did:
>
> "The Warren Court's noblest enterprise, school
> desegregation, and its most popular enterprise, re-
> apportionment, . . . are heading toward obsolescence
> and abandonment."

That is a fair indication of the boldness of Alex
Bickel's mind, and also of its breadth. He did not hesi-
tate to tackle the largest issues of law and public policy.
Nor did he mind finding himself on the side of the non-

angels, as some liberal-minded people thought from time to time. When a friend complained that Professor Bickel, by criticizing the *process* used to achieve some desirable political result, had given aid and comfort to the enemy, he wrote back: "How often have I been told that to say this or that is to give comfort to one or another s.o.b. I have generally functioned without regard to the question of aid and comfort."

Process is what especially concerned him—the relationship between the legal and the political process in a country where the two are uniquely intermixed. If he criticized something done by the courts for the stated purpose of speeding school desegregation, that did not mean that he favored state-imposed racial discrimination; in fact, he abhorred it. He was concerned, rather, about trying to solve complicated problems by legal formulas instead of leaving them to the give-and-take of the political process. The latter is sloppy and often frustrating, but he worried that tidiness in law might end as brittle rigidity.

In this book he spelled out his fear of rigid law in, among other areas, the highly sensitive one of race in schools. As a law clerk to Justice Frankfurter, he had played a part in the legal research that preceded judgment in *Brown* v. *Board of Education*. When the South resisted, he wrote in powerful support of the Supreme Court's conclusion that segregation-by-law violated the Constitution. But he came to see the problem as much more complex than a moral dilemma, involving such things as the relationship of cities and suburbs, the economic disparities between rich and poor school districts, the need for blacks to identify with schools in their own communities. He concluded that only the gradual working of the political system could deal with the school problem—a political system not bound by the Court's one-man, one-vote ruling and hence free to weight votes for social purposes. Viewing the reapportionment and school cases critically, as he did, he said he doubted the value of judicial intervention into "large areas of social policy."

In reading *The Supreme Court and the Idea of Progress*, one must remember that Alex Bickel had a zest for combat. He loved to provoke; he believed that provocation led to reexamination of assumptions and hence was a necessary if not sufficient prelude to wisdom. And unlike many persons of strong opinions, he welcomed criticism of his own views. Arguing with him in life was an intellectual adventure that could lead to the discovery of one's own beliefs, and reading the words he left behind should have the same effect. The point is that, however sharp his words—and he was a lawyer who made journalists blush for their clumsiness in expression—his real disapproval was not for any opposing principle but for lack of principle: for humbug, hypocrisy, unthinking subservience to power. Because of his doubts about the Warren Court, he was claimed by conservatives at the time of his death in 1974. In fact, he detested the unprincipled reaction that so often passes for conservatism in this age. He detested racism, the savage obsessiveness displayed in the Vietnam War, the love of secrecy and power in the White House. He was a conservative in the classic sense, believing that justice in any society depends on respect for the rules: respect by citizens, presidents, secretaries of state, and judges.

Candor—and the spirit of Alexander Bickel—require that I indicate where I disagree with his thesis in this book. I think the judicial role in deciding fundamental social questions has values that he underestimates. In a cynical age, courts at their best focus on issues of principle. In an age of bureaucracy and untraceable orders, judges remain personally responsible for their decisions and are obligated to explain what they do. In an age of remote, centralized power, courts are open in communities across the country to hear personally from those interested and to resolve issues local and national.

Specifically, I disagree with the negative view of the reapportionment cases. The rule of one-man, one-vote has not put a straitjacket on the political process; to the contrary, it has made politics more open and more responsive to accelerating change. Nor is there any lingering sign of resistance to the decision. On school segregation the judgment has to be more mixed. Without *Brown* v. *Board of Education,* it would have taken decades more to free the South from the self-inflicted grip of racism; Jimmy Carter could not have appeared when he did, in the politics of Georgia or the country. But we have certainly learned much about the limits of judicial wisdom in racial matters—as Professor Bickel foresaw.

Alex Bickel sometimes sounded as though he would

hold judges to a standard of perfection: Their vision must be perfect, or they should stay their hand from great social issues. In practice he was the opposite of absolute. He ended this book uncertain about the source and scope of judicial power but convinced that in our country it is necessary—so long as it keeps within limits. He devoted his genius to helping us find those limits.

Anthony Lewis

Preface

This volume is an expanded and documented version of the 1969 Oliver Wendell Holmes lectures, which I delivered at Harvard Law School on October 6, 7 and 8.

I take pleasure in recording my gratitude to Professor A. James Casner, Acting Dean of Harvard Law School in 1967–68; to Derek C. Bok, the present Dean; and to other old and new friends at Harvard, who did me the honor of calling me to the Holmes lectureship.

My colleagues Jan G. Deutsch, Abraham S. Goldstein, and Harry H. Wellington read portions of the manuscript, and made valuable suggestions. These I have heeded, and yet I am, of course, not entitled to assume that they agree with my thesis, or approve of my exposition of it. My colleague John G. Simon and I have for some years taught a course on public schools at the Yale Law School, and I have learned a great deal from him on this subject, with which I deal in Chapter 4. I am particularly indebted to him for making me see early on that the school decentralization movement in New York City was no passing fad. Needless to say, he too is not to be taxed with the positions I take.

I am very grateful also to Mrs. Alice Oliver for secretarial assistance, and to Mrs. Meira G. Pimsleur for an excellent index.

A. M. B.

New Haven
October, 1969

THE SUPREME COURT

AND THE IDEA

OF PROGRESS

Chapter 1

The Warren Court

Like so many of his predecessors, Earl Warren, fourteenth Chief Justice of the United States, gave his name to *a* Court. Article III of the Constitution established "one supreme Court," but we are prone to speak of many—a Marshall, a Taney, a Taft, and a Hughes Court, even a Chase and Vinson, and certainly a Warren Court. We seem incapable of possessing our past save in temporal segments. And the periods we impose on the history of the Supreme Court we call by the names of men, generally Chief Justices. No one man puts his exclusive stamp on the Court, but among all the men who do not, it is least invidious to regard the Chief Justice as if he did.

The practice is, on the whole, harmless enough, and often it achieves a certain aptness. Yet it is important to remember that other dates can be more crucial than those of the Chiefs. The battle in 1916 over the nomination of Louis D. Brandeis may more usefully be taken as the beginning of an age in the life of the Court than the accession to the Chief Justiceship of Edward Douglass White five years earlier, or of William Howard Taft five years later. So also the rejection of the nomination of John J. Parker as Associate Justice may have been a more telling event in 1930 than the assumption of the Chief Justiceship by Charles Evans Hughes, and certainly the Court-packing fight of 1937 was more decisive than Hughes's retirement in 1941. Even in the case of the Warren era, other dates demand to be recorded, as for example the retirement of Mr. Justice Frankfurter in 1962, which measurably contracted the universe of judicial discourse. But as much as most Courts called by the names of Chief Justices, and even, perhaps, more distinctly, the Warren Court existed, and it inhabited an era.

The era opened with *Brown* v. *Board of Education*, the school segregation case,[*][1] just a few months after Earl Warren took his seat, in sudden succession to Fred M. Vinson, who had died unexpectedly in the summer of 1953. The *Brown* case itself did not seem to represent a sharp break with the seven preceding Vinson years. Yet the appearance of continuity is superficial, and it is limited to racial cases. The Vinson Court had carried forward a process, begun under Chief Justice Hughes in the 1930's, of desegregating state institutions of higher learning,[2] it had dealt harshly with efforts to maintain the

[*] Superior numbers refer to Notes, page 182.

white primary,[3] and it had forbidden enforcement of racial covenants.[4] In a quite different exercise of judicial power, it had intervened spectacularly against President Truman's effort to settle a strike by seizing the steel industry.[5] But the segregation and voting decisions were not the dominant feature of the Vinson Court's record, and the *Steel Seizure Case* of 1952 was a singular and self-terminating episode. The two decisive opinions, among the many that the Court wrote, were those of Justices Frankfurter and Clark, and they were quite restricted.

It was more characteristic of the Vinson Court that all too often it supported, in a tone of avuncular patriotism, the loyalty-security mania and the xenophobia of the day.[6] In *Dennis* v. *United States*[7] it upheld, rather *con brio,* the power of government to punish seditious speech and association. In criminal cases, it could speak with the one-sided zeal of the prosecutor.[8] Far from entering new claims to judicial supremacy, it seemed at times to forget even its independence. The authentic Vinson Court manifested itself in its last act, the hurried special session at which it sealed the fates of Julius and Ethel Rosenberg, the so-called atom spies. The question that faced the Justices was whether meeting the latest schedule set for the Rosenbergs' execution was a more important objective than allowing time for the deliberate resolution of difficult legal problems of first impression. The Vinson Court met the schedule with a few hours to spare, although not without dissent.[9]

Against such a background, the Warren Court decided *Brown* v. *Board of Education.* The judges were plainly conscious of entering upon a great and intricate new enterprise. The evidence of this consciousness emerges in the opinion which announced the deliberate-speed formula, a year after the first decision of May 17, 1954.[10] And the perceptive listener could garner it at the three full arguments the Court allowed in *Brown* and its companion cases. He would have heard Mr. Justice Frankfurter probe the enforcement problem, worry about the possible gerrymandering of school districts that were supposedly not constituted on racial lines, and finally say: "Nothing could be worse from my point of view than for this Court to make an abstract declaration that segregation is bad and then have it evaded by tricks."[11] And the listener would have noted persistent indications of Mr. Justice Jackson's feeling that the issue before the Court was better left to the legislature, and that the ideal solution of it from the Court's point of view would be to find a formula for making precisely a sort of "abstract declaration" that would encourage Congress to deal with the problem under the enforcement clause of the Fourteenth Amendment.

The question, said Jackson to the future Justice Thurgood Marshall, then principal counsel for the Negro plaintiffs, was "the propriety of exercising judicial power to reach this result [the result Marshall was contending for] . . . in the absence of any [Congressional] legislation." To Assistant Attorney General J. Lee Rankin, arguing for the United States as *amicus* in support of the Negro plaintiffs, Jackson said: "Isn't the one thing that is perfectly clear under the Fourteenth Amendment that Congress is given the power and the duty to enforce the Fourteenth Amendment by legislation?" And identifying a consideration that was to become central to the Warren Court's conception of its function, Jackson added: "I suppose that realistically the reason this case is here is that action couldn't be obtained from Congress."[12]

Brown v. *Board of Education* was the beginning. Subsequently, the Court declared Bible reading and all other religious exercises in public schools unconstitutional;[13] it ordered the reapportionment of the national House of Representatives, of both houses of state legislatures, and of local government bodies on a one-man, one-vote basis;[14] it reformed numerous aspects of state and federal criminal procedure, significantly enhancing the rights of the accused, including juvenile offenders;[15] it held that wiretapping and eavesdropping are subject to the Fourth Amendment's prohibition against unreasonable searches and seizures, and that evidence obtained in violation of that prohibition may not be admitted in state or federal trials;[16] and it laid down a whole set of new rules governing the admissibility of confessions, and, in effect, the conduct of police throughout the country toward persons arrested on suspicion of crime.[17]

The Court also—needless to say, this listing is not comprehensive—enlarged its own jurisdiction to hear cases challenging federal expenditures,[18] expanded the concept of state action under the Fourteenth Amendment, thus enabling itself and Congress to reach and prohibit private discriminations not sponsored or initiated by state governments or their subdivisions,[19] and introduced a striking degree of permissiveness into the regulation—what is left of it—by state and federal authorities of material alleged to be obscene.[20] In addition, the Court

7

limited the power of state and federal government to forbid the use of birth-control devices,[21] to restrict travel,[22] to expatriate naturalized or native-born citizens,[23] to deny employment to persons whose associations are deemed subversive,[24] and to apply the laws of libel.[25]

The end of the Warren era was marked not only by the departure of the Chief Justice, but by an expression of disapproval, and an unusually pointed assertion of countervailing power, on the part of Congress in the Omnibus Crime Control and Safe Streets Act of 1968.[26] The change in the Chief Justiceship was accompanied, moreover, by the resignation of Justice Fortas, and may be followed by other new appointments within the span of a single Presidential administration. A final indication that an era had closed was that, as the Chief Justice left it, the Court confronted, with respect at least to public-school education and legislative apportionment, and in other fields as well, a new generation of problems.

Chapter 2

The Heavenly City of the Twentieth-Century Justices

"When eras die," runs a verse by Clarence Day, "their legacies/Are left to strange police./Professors in New England guard/The glory that was Greece." Professors in New England—and elsewhere, to be sure—parse the glories of the Warren Court, criticize its syllogisms, reduce its purported logic to absurd consequences, disprove its factual assertions, answer the unavoidable questions it managed to leave unasked, and most often conclude by regretting its failures of method, while either welcoming its results or professing detachment from them. Historians a generation or two hence, however—other professors in New England—may barely note, and care little about, method, logic, or intellectual coherence, and may assess results in hindsight—only results, and by their own future lights.

Past historians have so dealt with the Court, as do many—outside the profession, most—contemporary observers,* and one sensed that this was what the Justices of the Warren Court expected, and that they were content to take their chances.† They relied on events for vindication more than on the method of reason for contemporary validation. They were thoroughly conscious of the condemnation that has been visited on certain of their predecessors, who exalted rights of property, but responded with insufficient vigor to other claims, and they admired the generally admired force and vision of John Marshall,

* See, *e.g.*: "Only history will know whether the Warren Court has struck the balance right. For myself, I am confident that historians will write that the trend of decisions during the 1950's and 1960's was in keeping with the mainstream of American history—a bit progressive but also moderate, a bit humane but not sentimental, a bit idealistic but seldom doctrinaire and in the long run essentially pragmatic—in short, in keeping with the true genius of our institutions." Archibald Cox, *The Warren Court*, 133–34 (1968).

† Strictly speaking, the Justices of the Warren Court, in addition to the Chief Justice, were: Hugo L. Black, Stanley F. Reed, Felix Frankfurter, William O. Douglas, Robert H. Jackson, Harold H. Burton, Tom C. Clark, Sherman Minton, John M. Harlan, William J. Brennan, Jr., Charles E. Whittaker, Potter Stewart, Byron R. White, Arthur J. Goldberg, Abe Fortas, and Thurgood Marshall. In my usage, the terms "Warren Court" and "Justices of the Warren Court" refer to the dominant majority that gave the Court its character. That majority consisted over the years of the Chief Justice and Justices Black, Douglas, Brennan, Goldberg, Fortas, and Marshall. Of course, the majority was no monolith. There were defections, if that is the right word, in one or another case—on Justice Black's part, with increasing frequency toward the end—and the majority would now and then draw to itself a member of the opposition, if that, again, is the right word, such as Justice Stewart or Justice White. And in Brown v. Board of Education and a number of other racial cases, the Court was unanimous.

who is forgiven for his attachment to the rights of property. Like Marshall, who had, of course, the advantage of a clean slate, they bet on the future, even if to do so they had to wield, on their slate, eraser as well as chalk.

The eraser was used selectively, however, if often. For what informed the enterprise was the idea of progress. There was, therefore, discontinuity—open or disguised—in specifics, but there was also an aspiration to a transcendent consistency with a preferred past, a striving for fidelity to a true line of progress. And so the Warren Court, as Namier said we all do, "imagine[d] the past and remember[ed] the future."¹ The cast of mind is perhaps nowhere more saliently, more ingenuously—or more succinctly—exhibited than in a decisive remark of Mr. Justice Douglas, speaking for the Warren Court in one of the reapportionment cases. Said Justice Douglas: "The conception of political equality from the Declaration of Independence, to Lincoln's Gettysburg Address, to the Fifteenth, Seventeenth, and Nineteenth Amendments can mean only one thing—one person, one vote."² The key word is *can,* and the sentence is further notable for its references to documents not commonly taken as having legal effect, and to the extralegal significance of provisions that do have strictly legal, but circumscribed, application.

The Justices of the Warren Court thus ventured to identify a goal. It was necessarily a grand one—if we had to give it a single name, that name, as Professor Kurland has suggested,³ would be the Egalitarian Society. And the Justices steered by this goal, as Marshall did by his vision of a nation, in the belief that progress, called history, would validate their course, and that another generation, remembering its own future, would imagine them favorably. Such a faith need not conflict with, but it overrides standards of analytical reason and scientific inquiry as warrantors of the validity of judgment. On such a faith— if I may add another paraphrase to the title, and adapt the thesis of the late Carl L. Becker's brilliant disquisition on the great rationalist *philosophes*—on such a faith was built the Heavenly City of the Twentieth-Century Justices.*

Like the eighteenth-century philosophers of whom Becker wrote, our Justices followed a medieval age, which itself succeeded an earlier enlightenment, though they did not follow it immediately, since there was a period of transition. They, too, were rationalists coming after men of faith—most of them were rationalists; another classification is needed for Mr. Justice Black, and the term is at any rate presently to be qualified.

At the turn of the century, leaders of opinion consecrated the Constitution, and deified the judges who were the Constitution's supposed impersonal voices. In the midst of crisis in 1936, just before the crash, Justice George Sutherland recalled how he had been taught in youth that the Constitution "was a divinely inspired in-

---

* C. L. Becker, *The Heavenly City of the Eighteenth-Century Philosophers* (1932). I am aware of the criticism that Professor Peter Gay has leveled at Becker's "charming" book. See P. Gay, *The Party of Humanity*, 188–210 (1964). I think my own use of it is not vulnerable to the criticism. Becker's wit, Professor Gay charges, led him into exaggerations and excesses. On these my argument does not rely. And I do not adopt, I trust, Becker's tone—if such it be—of impatience and of diminished respect; I portray my *philosophes* neither as "naïve," nor as "a little fraudulent," to quote Professor Gay's accusation against Becker.

14

strument." He added: "I truly think it is."[4] Justice David J. Brewer was uttering no mere pleasantry, although he spoke with a touch of affectionate irony, when he said of his colleague John Marshall Harlan the Elder in 1902 that Harlan "believes implicitly in the Constitution. He goes to bed every night with one hand on the Constitution and the other on the Bible, and so sleeps the sweet sleep of justice and righteousness. He believes in the Constitution as it was written; that the Constitution as it was must be the Constitution as it is, and the Constitution as it shall be. . . . To him it is no rope of sand to be broken by every legislative mandate, nor cord of rubber to be stretched by any tension of popular feeling. . . ."[5] Not the remotest trace of irony infected this much-quoted *te deum*, as Ralph H. Gabriel called it, sung in 1913 by Henry R. Estabrook of the New York Bar: "Our great and sacred Constitution, serene and inviolable, stretches its beneficent powers over our land . . . like the outstretched arm of God himself . . . the people of the United States . . . ordained and established one Supreme Court—the most rational, considerate, discerning, veracious, impersonal power—the most candid, unaffected, conscientious, incorruptible power. . . . O Marvellous Constitution! Magic Parchment! Transforming Word! Maker, Monitor, Guardian of Mankind!"[6]

Such was the style of the old faith. The substance was an unyielding assertion of judicial supremacy, to be exerted in defense of the rights of property and the freedom of individual enterprise. A major component of the intellectual climate in which these beliefs flourished was a deeply anti-egalitarian Social Darwinism, optimistic in its

Spencerian confidence that the progress of society inhered in the nature of things, but imbued with a terrible pessimism about man's capacity to move purposefully in the right direction[7] (except, perhaps, as the captains of business knew how to manage business, and how, if need be, to rationalize the economy).

The democratic ideal was, of course, scarcely in vogue. The political system as it existed was acceptable—the entrepreneurs had learned to manipulate it reasonably well—but it was little more than a necessary evil. Elbert H. Gary, chairman of U.S. Steel, publicly voiced the conviction—in a Congressional hearing, at that—not only that "the salvation of the country really is in the courts," but also that all government should be above politics, that "one of the great disturbers and objections to the conditions and proceedings of this country is the frequent elections," and that "even the President of the United States, after he is elected [a necessary concession, there] . . . [should be] absolutely independent."[8] Gary's views—Judge Gary, he was called, having served on a county court in Illinois—may not have been typical, as his candor certainly was not, but they represented a tendency.

Style and substance, to be sure, medium and message, were not always one. There were deviations in both. The same Justice Harlan, for example, who believed so implicitly in the unalterable Constitution and who did his share to protect property, also had a streak of populism in him. And for about a decade before the First World War, as the Progressive movement reached the height of its political effectiveness, the Court as a whole trimmed on the substance of its faith. The judges, it briefly seemed, knew, as Tocqueville said they must, "how to understand the spirit of the age, to confront those obstacles that can be overcome, and to steer out of the current when the tide threatens to carry them away."[9]

It got so that some Progressives were beginning to speak in praise of the Court's "fitness to apply the Constitution to American life."[10] Just as the Vinson Court stepped essentially out of character to upset President Truman's strike-settling seizure of the steel industry, so the White Court in 1917 strained to uphold, on the narrowest ground possible, President Wilson's settlement of a railroad strike, even though government regulation of hours of labor, and indirectly also of wages, was involved.[11] But, throughout this period, there was no change in the dominant style of judging. And the period was brief and it passed. A reunion of style and substance soon followed.

Stylistic deviations, a certain private cynicism about the prevalent consecration and deification, accompanied by the most unflinching adherence to substance, also occurred, most commonly among politicians. As late as 1922, William Howard Taft, by then Chief Justice, warmly disagreed with Brandeis' assertion that in choosing judges Presidents necessarily looked to a man's "views as to property." We can't, said Taft—he meant we needn't —"go round looking for men with certain creeds on property."[12] But there were those who did fortify the faith by seeking the appointment as judges of "men with certain creeds on property." Stalwart Republicans in 1910, for example, preferred White to Hughes as Chief Justice because they did not trust Hughes' adherence to the creed. "I said to [Senator Elihu] Root yesterday," reported the very conservative Senator Francis E. Warren of Wyoming, "I am not feeling very bad about White's being made Chief Justice instead of Hughes. Root replied, I am very happy over it. White [who was a Louisiana Democrat] is a better Republican than Hughes. He is an old-fashioned Federalist and a straight-forward, fair man. Nobody can vouch for Hughes' politics."[13]

It will have been noted that the *te deum* by Henry Estabrook that I quoted a moment ago praised the Court as rational, among other probable and improbable attributions. But it is no sort of paradox for such a proclamation of faith to include also an appeal to reason. "The function of intelligence" in the medieval world, wrote Carl Becker, was "to demonstrate the truth of revealed knowledge, to reconcile diverse and pragmatic experience with the rational pattern of the world as given in faith."[14] The age of reason, Voltaire's age, was called so because it applied reason quite differently, to the end of denying and disproving the prior faith—but only in order to substitute another, ultimately not entirely dissimilar; no longer Christianity, not the Heavenly City of St. Augustine, but nature and progress.

So also, beginning with Holmes's scholarly writings and John Chipman Gray's, and shortly before the First World War with such books as J. Allen Smith's *The Spirit of American Government* (1907), and Charles A. Beard's *The Supreme Court and the Constitution* (1912) and *An Economic Interpretation of the Constitution* (1913), and later in the work of the American legal realists, as some named themselves, reason brought down the old constitutional faith. Its style was exploded, and its substance exposed and rejected. But faith as such was not banished; reason was not enthroned in solitary sovereignty. Optimism about progress inhering in the nature of things and pessimism about man's capacity himself to move things along in the right direction—these two attitudes changed places, so to speak, so that men now feared deterioration in social and economic conditions that were left unattended, and acquired confidence in their own capacity to change their environment and institutional arrangements for the better. To the extent that progress is man-made, however, the discovery of its proper direction is crucial, and that discovery would at some stage be seen to be quite as much an act of faith as the optimistic reliance on automatic progress.* Belief in man-made progress was the new faith, and the supremacy of judges as its carriers and executors was not denied. The Justices of the Warren Court were the children of these Progressive realists— again allowing an exception to Justice Black, whose achievement it has been to adapt the old style to a substance of his own.

For the Progressive realists, the Constitution was not a catechism, and the judges were not priests reciting it. They demanded of the judges an understanding "of the great industrial and political problems now before us" and

---

* Progress, says Bury, "belongs to the same order of ideas as Providence or personal immortality [which, of course, are the ideas it displaced]. It is true or it is false, and like them it cannot be proved either true or false. Belief in it is an act of faith." J. B. Bury, *The Idea of Progress*, 4 (1932).

"sympathy with the big movements which have for their aim the promotion of the public welfare."[15] Law, said Felix Frankfurter in 1915, is "a vital agency for human betterment,"[16] and constitutional law, he had said a couple of years earlier, on the grand occasion of the *Harvard Law Review*'s twenty-fifth anniversary banquet, is "applied politics, using the word in its noble sense."[17] The judges had to be "equal to fashioning ideas and instruments with which to make the accommodations necessary for a gracious civilization"[18]—no less, one is tempted to comment.

In 1922, in an unpublished passage that, he said, expressed his strong conviction, although he omitted it from a dissenting opinion at the behest of a colleague, Brandeis wrote: "Our Constitution is not a strait-jacket. It is a living organism. As such it is capable of growth—of expansion and of adaptation to new conditions. Growth implies changes, political, economic, and social. Growth which is significant manifests itself rather in intellectual and moral conceptions than in material things."[19] For his part, Thomas Reed Powell, a rationalist of rationalists, laid great stress on "practical wisdom."[20] "This in a nutshell is my thesis," he wrote: "The logic of constitutional law is the common sense of the Supreme Court of the United States."[21] In a word, the judges were to be statesmen, as in the earlier enlightenment Tocqueville had called them,[22] and they were much preached to about facts, human experience, the scientific method, change and progress.

Even so did the eighteenth-century philosophers preach, but Becker was driven to ask whether they were

not actually "engaged in that nefarious medieval enterprise of reconciling the facts of human experience with
truths already, in some fashion, revealed to them" and to
answer, "Alas yes, that is, indeed, the fact!"[23] While they
were on the attack, dismantling the old religious order,
and also during a transitional interlude after they had
come to power in the late 1930's, the legal realists had
little need to ask Becker's question of themselves, for the
judges were not called upon to reform society or to stop
the wrong kind of change. They were not called upon to
enact progress, but merely to allow it; others, legislators
and executives, would enact it. Hence a new, scientific
style and the repudiation of the old belief in the sanctity
of property and the freedom of enterprise were sufficient*
to secure the overthrow of such decisions as *Lochner* v.
New York,[24] in which the Court had held, in 1905, that
maximum-hours legislation was unconstitutional.

It was merely as a hedge against what might come
after, as a prudent qualification—and, to be sure, because

---

* In 1917, in the second dissenting opinion of his career, against a
decision striking down a state regulation of employment agencies,
Brandeis wrote that the Court's "assumptions and *a priori* reasoning" could not be allowed to determine the result. "The judgment
should be based upon a consideration of relevant facts, actual or
possible—*Ex facto jus oritur*. That ancient rule must prevail in order
that we may have a system of living law." Adams v. Tanner, 244
U.S. 590, 597, 600 (1917). A few years later, in a passage at once
more blunt and somewhat more wary, he said in another dissent:
"Knowledge is essential to understanding; and understanding should
precede judging. Sometimes, if we would guide by the light of reason, we must let our minds be bold. But, in this case, we have
merely to acquaint ourselves with the art of breadmaking and the
uses of the trade." Burns Baking Co. v. Bryan, 264 U.S. 504, 517,
520 (1924).

21

he himself did not particularly share the belief in man-made progress—that Holmes suggested, "timidly," he said, to Felix Frankfurter in 1923, "caution in the use of the word statesmanship with regard to judges. Of course, it is true that considerations of the same class come before their minds that have to be or ought to be the motives of legislators, but the word suggests a more political way of thinking than is desirable and also has become slightly *banal*. I didn't think the late Chief Justice [White, that was] shone most when he was political. . . . When economic views affect judicial action I should prefer to give such action a different name from that which I should apply to the course of Wilson or Lodge."[25]

Economic views were still chiefly in question, but Holmes perceived that the new style—his style—could for others bring a new substance in its train. And the upshot would be conflict with political democracy, which was a strongly-held tenet of the Progressive realists, and with the pragmatic skepticism that was also part of their intellectual make-up. The Progressives and the legal realists were no Jacksonian democrats, and they were not to be confused with the agrarian populists with whom they were at times loosely allied. But they all—even the otherwise Hamiltonian Theodore Roosevelt—put great store by political democracy. None would be heard to speak of elections in the accents of Elbert H. Gary. A legacy of the age, after all, is the political reforms aimed at achieving more consistently majoritarian government. So the Progressive realists viewed the policy-making function of judges as deviant in a democratic society. Their experience with the consecrated Constitution—"Maker, Monitor, Guardian of Mankind"—had rendered them skeptical, moreover, of claims to generality and permanence entered in behalf of social and economic principles. On this score also they preferred policy evolved through the political process.

Frankfurter, thoroughly Progressive and democratic and adequately skeptical, heeded the Holmesian caution, both before and after Holmes suggested it to him. He never succumbed to the vulgar cynicism that came to afflict some of his fellow realists in later years. If constitutional law was applied politics, it was politics in its noble sense, employing the method of reason as far as it could be pushed and not played with an eye to personal or partisan advantage; principled politics, not the garden-variety art of the possible. But constitutional law *was* applied politics; constitutional adjudication *was* a task of statesmanship.

There came a time when the caution was no longer merely a prudent hedge, when its meaning was of the essence, because the judges were invited themselves to define progress, and to use reason, not in the demolition of an earlier Heavenly City, but in their own rehearsal of "that nefarious medieval enterprise of reconciling the facts of human experience with truths already, in some fashion, revealed to them." For Holmes in his most frequently dominant mood ("here lies the supple tool of power"),[26] the temptation was easily resisted, the invitation readily declined; he would simply leave the work of progress to others. But Brandeis and Frankfurter, while democrats and pragmatists, were also moralists and reformers. They tried valiantly to avoid getting caught in

23

the old medieval enterprise, and to find the necessary revealed truths by the method of reason elsewhere than in themselves. They sought the truths they needed in the past. Like the eighteenth-century philosophers, they soon saw, however, that the past had to be imagined if it was to be of any use. And they sought their truths in the pronouncements of other institutions. But these were simply not always satisfactory, and were indeed sometimes intolerable.

Again and again, on and off the bench, Frankfurter counseled candor, an open and realistic appreciation of the judicial function, so that, at the least, there would be disclosure of just which *a priori* truths human experience was being reconciled to. The Justices, he wrote in 1934, were compelled "to gather meaning not from reading the constitution but from reading life. . . . [T]he process of constitutional interpretation compels the translation of policy into judgment, and the controlling conceptions of the justices are their 'idealized political picture' of the existing social order. Only the conscious recognition of the nature of this exercise of the judicial process will protect policy from being narrowly construed as the reflex of discredited assumptions or the abstract formulation of unconscious bias."[27]

But the conscious recognition of the nature of the exercise would not always succeed in keeping discredited (discredited in whose eyes?) assumptions out of the Constitution, and it scarcely discouraged introduction of other principles and revealed truths, from which Frankfurter himself might have withheld the pejorative appellation "assumptions." Policy made by judges who were conscious of what they were doing might be more suitable to the present state of society, but it would still be policy made by judges—undemocratic and often rigid.

One solution was to cut the Gordian knot, drastically to reduce the judicial function by eliminating, or limiting very strictly, the most broadly-worded provisions of the Constitution. Judicial statesmanship would then, for the most part, consist of fidelity to legislative policy. Both Frankfurter and Brandeis—as at a later date, Learned Hand[28]—at one time proposed this solution. Frankfurter, in 1925, in a well-known article entitled "Can the Supreme Court Guarantee Toleration?", welcomed the decisions in *Meyer* v. *Nebraska,*[29] *Bartels* v. *Iowa,*[30] and *Pierce* v. *Society of Sisters*[31] (all concurred in by Brandeis, Holmes dissenting in the first two). In *Meyer* and *Bartels* the Supreme Court struck down statutes that forbade the teaching of foreign languages to children under a certain age. In *Pierce* it declared unconstitutional an Oregon law that in effect closed down parochial and other private schools by forcing all children between the ages of eight and sixteen to attend the public schools. These decisions, Frankfurter wrote, put a salutary end to an "effort to regiment the mental life of Americans." But he added: "In rejoicing . . . we must not forget that a heavy price has to be paid for these occasional services to liberalism." The same constitutional words, the Due Process Clauses, "whose contents are derived from the disposition of the Justices," produced and could continue to produce decisions like *Lochner* v. *New York*. The cost, he concluded, was on the whole greater than the gain.[32]

About a year earlier, Frankfurter had exclaimed in the

New Republic: "The due process clauses ought to go."[33]
And at about the same time, in a conversation of which
Frankfurter has left us a record, he and Brandeis drove
each other to the conclusion that the Due Process Clauses
should be repealed, or at any rate, as Brandeis also suggested publicly from the bench, restricted to procedural
matters.[34]

This might have been a solution, since a great deal of
policy made autonomously by judges is made under cover
of the vague and ample Due Process Clauses.* But, alas,
as Becker might have said, this solution was in the end unacceptable. While the Due Process Clauses remained,
Brandeis and Frankfurter agreed, "they must be applied
to substantive law and so as to things which are fundamental," among which they enumerated the "right to
speech," the "right to education"—in part a reference, no
doubt, to the problem of the *Meyer, Bartels,* and *Pierce*
cases—the "right to choice of profession," and the "right to
locomotion." These rights were "not to be impaired or

* The Due Process Clauses, quite aside from their technical cover-
age, which is vast enough in itself, also symbolized for Frankfurter
and Brandeis the policy-making power of judges in general. In the
text that follows, Frankfurter and Brandeis discuss the problem of
free speech. The applicable constitutional provision in federal cases
is the First Amendment. In state cases, it is the Due Process Clause
of the Fourteenth Amendment. Frankfurter and Brandeis might at
the time have thought there was more historical warrant for the
exercise of judicial power under the First Amendment than under
the Due Process Clause of the Fourteenth. But Frankfurter did not
long continue to hold to that view. And Brandeis demonstrated that
he would do under the Due Process Clause of the Fourteenth
Amendment what he thought should be done as well under the First
Amendment. The *Meyer, Bartels* and *Pierce* cases were decided
under the Due Process Clause.

withdrawn except as judged by the 'clear and present danger' test."

Holmes was against extending the Fourteenth Amendment, Brandeis reported. But that meant, Brandeis said, that "you are going to cut down freedom through striking down regulation of property, but not give protection [to freedom in other contexts]." It was "absurd," as Holmes said, to hold property "fundamental in the sense that you can't curtail its use or its accumulations of power." There might be some aspects of property that were fundamental, but Brandeis did not so regard "specific limitations upon it, whereas the right to your education or to utter speech is fundamental, *except* clear and present danger." And even that qualification disturbed Brandeis. "I have never been quite happy about my concurrence in the *Debs*[35] and *Schenck*[36] cases," he said to Frankfurter on another occasion. These were the cases, arising during World War I, in which the Espionage Act of 1917 was applied to punish anti-war and anti-conscription speeches and publications. And it was in these cases that Holmes evolved the clear-and-present-danger test.

"I had not then thought the issues of freedom of speech out," Brandeis continued. "I thought at the subject, not through it. Not until I came to write [in] the *Pierce* and *Schaefer* cases did I understand it." *Pierce* v. *United States*[37] and *Schaefer* v. *United States*[38] were somewhat later prosecutions under the Espionage Act, which came up for decision after the war. Brandeis and Holmes dissented. "I would have placed the *Debs* case on the war power," Brandeis said, "instead of taking Holmes' line about 'clear and present danger.' Put it frankly on the war power . . . and then the scope of espionage legislation would be confined to war. But in peace the protection against restrictions on freedom of speech would be unabated." During a war, after all, one might as well recognize, all bets were off. "I didn't know enough in the early cases to put it on that ground. . . . But in the *Schaefer* and *Pierce* cases I made up my mind I would put it all out, let the future know what we weren't allowed to say in the days of the war and following."[39]

So the flirtation with abandonment of the Due Process Clauses was just that—a flirtation. More real was an assertion of fundamentals, and the claim upon the future for vindication. Even the old fundamentals that they had done so much to discredit received from both Holmes and Brandeis, as Justice Frankfurter once pointed out,[40] an occasional affirmation. "The best defense" for "leaving fundamental responsibilities to this Court," Holmes wrote to Frankfurter in 1921, "came from Brandeis [interestingly enough, not from himself] . . . —that constitutional restrictions enable a man to sleep at night and know that he won't be robbed before morning—which, in days of legislative activity and general scheming, otherwise he scarcely would feel sure about."[41]

It was with rather telling reservations, then, that the Progressive realists rejected faith, and as rationalists proclaimed what they were fond of calling the science of law. The reservations were for the most part theoretical and privately held; expressed, if at all, with their full import, in the closet, as by Brandeis and Frankfurter. There was little occasion to voice them otherwise. Professor Louis L. Jaffe has recently offered something of a reassessment of

Brandeis.[42] He observes that in joining the majority in *Meyer* v. *Nebraska* and *Pierce* v. *Society of Sisters,* the education cases mentioned earlier, and in his ringing dissents in *Olmstead* v. *United States,*[43] the wire-tapping case, and in *Whitney* v. *California*[44] and a few other free-speech cases, Brandeis insisted on his own set of fundamentals. He thus publicly aired the reservations that he and Frankfurter discussed privately. Yet, for the most part, these reservations could, with Brandeis, remain theoretical. Frankfurter, who sat as a judge well past the transitional years into the Warren era, had continually to grapple with them. He is the crucial figure, his is the paradigmatic career in modern American constitutional law. He was both witness and actor, a most active witness and most self-conscious actor, maker, chronicler, and executor of an intellectual revolution, participant both in its consummation and in its predicament.

As a judge, Frankfurter, like Brandeis before him, but more frequently and more painfully, deferred in two senses; in many instances he deferrred judgment, or in rendering judgment he deferred to the political institutions. "Courts are not representative bodies. They are not designed to be a good reflex of a democratic society," he said in 1951, concurring, in *Dennis* v. *United States,* in the decision that the anti-Communist Smith Act did not violate the First Amendment. He went on in the last paragraph of that opinion to paraphrase, and in places to use verbatim, passages from his 1925 article on the *Meyer* and *Pierce* cases, in which he had answered negatively the question "Can the Supreme Court Guarantee Toleration?" "Civil liberties," he wrote again in the *Dennis* opinion, after nearly a quarter of a century, "draw at best only limited strength from legal guaranties. Preoccupation by our people with the constitutionality, instead of with the wisdom, of legislation or of executive action is preoccupation with a false value. . . . Focusing attention on constitutionality tends to make constitutionality synonymous with wisdom. When legislation touches freedom of thought and freedom of speech, such a tendency is a formidable enemy of the free spirit. . . . The ultimate reliance for the deepest needs of civilization must be found outside their vindication in courts of law; apart from all else, judges, howsoever they may conscientiously seek to discipline themselves against it, unconsciously are too apt to be moved by the deep undercurrents of public feeling. A persistent, positive translation of the liberating faith into the feelings and thoughts and actions of men and women is the real protection against attempts to straitjacket the human mind."[45]

Frankfurter set apart, as fittingly exercised by judges, the Commerce Clause jurisdiction, in which judgments denying power to the States are subject to Congressional revision. He viewed as entirely justifiable as well, and separable, the function formulated by James Bradley Thayer, following the Marshall of *McCulloch* v. *Maryland*,[46] of guarding against capricious, and in this sense irrational legislation, whether state or national. The very statement of this function implied the heaviest possible presumption of constitutionality, and its exercise, when, rarely, the need for it arose, could be controlled by a process of factual and analytical inquiry.

Elsewhere, Frankfurter avoided the assertion of judicial

supremacy by resorting to devices such as statutory construction, which leave a reprise open to the legislature. If driven to ultimate constitutional judgment, he would seek to confine it to the interstitial—judgment at retail, in small compass. He inveighed against the postulation of absolutes by anyone, most of all by judges. He had studied as a young man, and often acknowledged the influence of, John Morley's *On Compromise*. His copy of the 1901 printing of the second edition is heavily annotated in a young man's version of his mature handwriting. And so he practiced—in his judicial capacity—a "wise suspense in forming opinions, wise reserve in expressing them, and wise tardiness in trying to realise them."[47]

Despite its title, however, *On Compromise* is chiefly a tract against intellectual "disingenuousness and self-illusion . . . voluntary dissimulation . . . indolence and pusillanimity," against "a flaccid latitudinarianism, which . . . is in truth only a pretentious form of being without settled opinions of our own, and without any desire to settle them."[48] No absolutes, therefore, as Holmes and Santayana also taught, and prudence in the imposition of one's principles on the society at large; yet certainly not an absence of settled opinions, and no unlimited readiness to sacrifice them when they were directly and inescapably challenged. The independence of the judge, and also a certain autonomy, Frankfurter upheld.

On the Vinson Court he was often in dissent, not least of all when the Court most blatantly hazarded its independence in *Rosenberg* v. *United States*.* [49] Criminal

* See *supra,* p. 5.

procedure generally raised for him issues of independence, of "the integrity of the judicial process."[50] He had
greeted *Powell* v. *Alabama*,[51] the Scottsboro Boys case of
1932, in which a right to be assigned counsel in criminal
prosecutions was established, with no such misgivings as
he had expressed about *Meyer* v. *Nebraska* and *Pierce* v.
*Society of Sisters.** It was, unqualifiedly, "a notable
chapter in the history of liberty." Any "uniform code of
criminal procedure federally imposed" would be unfortunate, but there was no question that basic matters of
criminal procedure were ultimately the province of
judges.[52]

It took no violent stretching of democratic theory to
suppose an expectation on the part of the people that, in
employing the criminal sanction, the political branches
would abide the judge's sense of what was mete and
decent in the way of procedure, just as they abided the
discretion of the jury. And, if the supposition concerning
popular expectations should prove wrong, then the justification of the judicial function was that criminal procedure,
and police behavior in general, too,[53] raised questions
of elemental justice to the individual, not of social policy.
Procedural safeguards, Frankfurter liked to think, moreover, were relatively well-defined by a less than usually
imagined past. So also—indeed more precisely defined
both by its formulation and its history—was the Fifteenth
Amendment's guarantee of racial equality in the exercise
of the franchise. But in substantive Due Process and
Equal Protection cases under the Fourteenth Amendment

* See *supra*, p. 25.

as well, outside the safer realms of procedure and of the Fifteenth Amendment, Frankfurter came on occasion to act the creative statesman—rarely, self-consciously, and almost in anguish, yet not, after the anguish, hesitantly.

He concurred, of course, in *Brown* v. *Board of Education,* and when the inner history of that case is known, we may find that he was a moving force in its decision. He was one of the masons who would have erected a wall of separation between church and state in parochial school-busing and released-time cases.[54] It is arguable to the point of being very likely, as Miss Helen Shirley Thomas has shown,[55] that his famous opinions upholding legislative authority to require a flag salute from schoolchildren whose parents objected to it on grounds of conscience[56] are explained, not merely by a reluctance, as in *Dennis,* to assert judicial supremacy, but by the very conception of the role of the public schools as secular, nationalizing agencies that underlay his position on public busing for parochial pupils and on released-time programs.

In *Sweezy* v. *New Hampshire,*[57] he held unconstitutional an effort by the state to interrogate a lecturer at the state university about the subject of a lecture and about his political affiliations and associations. This is an opinion of the first importance. The great statements of abnegation, such as the concurrence in *Dennis,* must not be read in isolation from it. He was performing, Frankfurter said in *Sweezy,* "the inescapable judicial task in giving substantive content, legally enforced, to the Due Process Clause, and it is a task ultimately committed to this Court."[58]

33

He always differentiated skillfully and resourcefully the many tasks that fall to the Court, he refined and invented techniques for deciding cases without assuming the supreme function of "giving substantive content, legally enforced, to the Due Process Clause," and he taught by numerous example how and how often these techniques are to be employed. But he taught also that, as he said again in *Sweezy,* "in the end, judgment cannot be escaped —the judgment of this Court."[39] Yet he never successfully identified sources from which this judgment was to be drawn that would securely limit as well as nourish it, he never achieved a rigorous general accord between judicial supremacy and democratic theory, so that the boundaries of the one could be described with some precision in terms of the other, and he was thus unable to ensure that the teaching of a duty of judgment would be received as subordinate to the teaching of abstention, for the relationship between the two is itself a matter for the judgment of statesmen.

Both teachings were his, unresolved from the beginning. His posterity was free to receive both. It inhered in the Court's past, in contemporary demands upon it, and perhaps in the iron laws of power that the teaching of the duty of judgment, although more an undertone than the dominant note in Frankfurter's work seen as a whole, was destined to have the more willing reception.

Despite much urging, and despite its attractiveness to others, he did not take what would have been an easy and more than a little sophistical way out of the dilemma in apportionment and political-speech cases. In such cases, it is often argued, there is no conflict with democratic theory, since the Court enhances, rather than derogating from, the democratic process. But the argument is question begging. With respect to the apportionment problem, the question whether one or another method of constructing a legislative institution is more democratic is the very question for decision. A simplistically populist answer begs it, and is in itself incomplete—are legislatures to be districted, is minority representation necessary, and how is it to be assured? A resolution of the problem that will enhance the democratic process is far from obvious if the slightest degree of complexity is allowed to infect populist assumptions. The issue then is one of the distribution of access and power among various groups, and the answer requires normative choices and prophetic judgments— much as does the solution of other problems of social policy.

A coup d'état abolishing elections and representative institutions or excluding an immutably and arbitrarily defined group from the political process would be something else again. And so would a measure flatly forbidding political speech and association. But the former has not been the occasion of the apportionment cases that have come to the Court, nor the latter of the free-speech cases.

The speech controversies have concerned utterances or associations thought by a legislature to be aimed at and to incite action that the legislature was concededly authorized to forbid, such as forcible overthrow of the government; or utterances and associations that in a given place and set of circumstances impinged on other, again concededly legitimate, interests of the society, such as the privacy of the individual or the peace and order of the

35

community; or indirect consequences for free speech and association flowing from the legislature's exercise of its power to set qualifications for office or other employments.

The values associated with freedom of utterance and of political action are assuredly touched on and perhaps abridged in such cases, but the viability of a democratic political process is hardly in question, unless one assumes the value of speech to be an absolute, totally coterminous with the democratic process. Short of such a heroic solution, the political-speech cases also call for normative choices and prophetic judgments, like obscenity, or privacy, or freedom-of-religion cases, and like the run of Due Process and Equal Protection controversies. When the judicial choices and judgments have been made, they may be thought good and hence called democratic. But the word can be used only in the sense in which it serves as a general term of praise for any wise and moderate accommodation between conflicting values and interests. Actually, the legislatures which made the contrary choices and judgments operated within the democratic political process, and it may with equal justification be thought that the Court damaged that process by withdrawing from its institutions the power to protect or promote interests that the community wishes to see protected or promoted.

To be sure, in both apportionment and speech cases, a group which has lost out in the political process—and may in this sense be called a minority—is asking the Court to arbitrate between it and the ruling majority. But that is always true, in all manner of cases. It was certainly true in all the old property and free-enterprise controversies. The best defense, Holmes said Brandeis thought, "for leaving fundamental responsibilities to this Court" was that constitutional restrictions enabled minorities to get an untroubled night's sleep. And the best defense for not leaving fundamental responsibilities to the Court is that the political process should rule. In the political process, groups sometimes lose out, but so long as the process is operational* and both diffuses power and allows majorities ultimately to work their will, no group that is prepared to enter into the process and combine with others need remain permanently and completely out of power.

The contention in the apportionment cases was, in effect, that there had been a coup, and that the majority was deprived of power, but it was a specious contention, as at least the Colorado case showed, since in Colorado the apportionment had been approved in a popular referendum.[60] Actually, a group of indeterminate size and momentarily insufficient political power or energy was appealing to the Court, and that is what always happens. In apportionment and free-speech cases as elsewhere, if such a group, which may handily be called a minority in the sense that it did not prevail politically, is to win its lawsuit, it must do so by getting the Court to revise a decision arrived at by the democratic process.

Frankfurter was unpersuaded that judicial supremacy

* It was not, of course, for many decades, operational so far as Southern Negroes were concerned, and that despite the Fifteenth Amendment, which purported to enfranchise them in 1870. Yet in the late 1950's and in the 1960's, Negro political power was felt, even in the South, and even before the Voting Rights Act of 1965 truly did enfranchise large numbers.

in apportionment and political-speech cases was specially justifiable; he could not convince himself that the judicial process functioned differently or produced different consequences in these cases, as compared with the general run of Due Process and Equal Protection litigation. Besides, all that was offered in this fashion was a partial, *ad hoc* escape from the dilemma of judicial supremacy. Other rights that Brandeis and Frankfurter had enumerated in their conversation also had claims to vindication. Should they be left in limbo, or should the speciousness of the argument be further extended, and should the judges tell themselves that, *ex hypothesi,* they enhance the democratic process whenever they vindicate what they view as fundamental rights? That would be to wring all meaning out of the concept of political democracy, and to win the game by sweeping the chessmen off the board.

Better to recognize candidly that judicial judgment was statesmanship superimposed on the democratic political process, and its final test was the future. So Frankfurter taught. The judge, he wrote in 1954—albeit extra-judicially, not in an opinion—had to be historian, philosopher, and prophet. Even though ill equipped to do so (the task requires "poetic sensibilities" and "the gift of imagination"), he must "pierce the curtain of the future . . . give shape and visage to mysteries still in the womb of time." He must "have antennae registering feeling and judgment beyond logical, let alone quantitative, proof."[61]

Speaking generally, therefore, and reserving judgment on the validity, wisdom, and worth of various judicial judgments, one can hardly tax Frankfurter's younger colleagues and his successors for seeing themselves in the role of statesmen discharging a responsibility for the progress of society. It was their fate, wished on them by the great men, chief among them, over a career of fifty years, Felix Frankfurter, who gave us an age of reason in American law, who disestablished an old faith and made room for a new.

The style of the new faith, like that of the old, is not always or universally adhered to. Thus in 1968, Justice Fortas, when asked by the chairman of the Senate Committee on the Judiciary, holding hearings on his abortive nomination as Chief Justice, "to what extent and under what circumstance" he believed "that the Court should attempt to bring about social, economic or political changes," replied: "Zero, absolutely zero." It is owing to Mr. Fortas to add that he had just remarked that, while the language of the Constitution is controlling, phrases like "due process of law" have no clear and unmistakable meaning. Yet Mr. Fortas said also that he did not believe the Court "should or can appropriately make policy."[62]

And there is, as we have noted earlier, Mr. Justice Black, magnificent in great age, and wedded to the sacred text of the Constitution—"the Constitution as it was must be the Constitution as it is"—no less than the elder Harlan. In 1966, declaring state poll taxes unconstitutional, the Court remarked that "[n]otions of what constitutes equal treatment for purposes of the Equal Protection Clause *do* change," and it compared *Brown* v. *Board of Education* with *Plessy* v. *Ferguson*. But Justice Black would have none of keeping "the Constitution up to date." He replied to the Court in the poll-tax case that he had not voted to abolish segregation in the public schools "on

39

any such theory." In his judgment, "the holding in *Brown* against racial discrimination was compelled by the purpose of the Framers of the Thirteenth, Fourteenth and Fifteenth Amendments completely to outlaw discrimination against people because of their race or color."[63] If Justice Black brought to the Constitution an unbending "self-assertive subjectivism," to use—most fittingly it seems to me—Richard Hofstadter's phrase about Andrew Jackson,[64] that was long ago, and it was not a self-conscious process; no more self-conscious as Justice Black's zest for progress waned than when, earlier, it waxed. But these were aberrant or fugitive attitudes in the day of statesmanship informed by the judicial intuition of progress.

There was much that was novel about the Warren Court, as compared with all its predecessors as well as its immediate one, not least of all the velocity it achieved over its last decade; although no more than surface novelty, if that, is likely to be found in the Warren Court's supposed imposition of affirmative norms on the society, as contrasted with the merely negative restraints interposed by earlier Courts against the initiatives of legislatures and executives. I have tried to trace the Warren Court's line of intellectual descent—descent or ascent in the terms of the Arkansas "anti-evolution" statute recently declared unconstitutional*—without regard, for the moment, to novelties and mutations that might have been

---

* "It shall be unlawful . . . to teach the theory or doctrine that mankind ascended or descended from a lower order of animals." Ark. Stat. Ann., 1947, § 80–1627. See Epperson v. Arkansas, 393 U.S. 97 (1968).

avoided, without regard to what may be thought not only novel, but wrong and self-defeating about the Court's work. Like the eighteenth-century philosophers in leaving Christianity behind, we have traveled a long distance from the constitutional religion of eighty and thirty years ago, but we have traveled in an arc. On a linear plane we are not so far from where we started. The distance is from *Lochner* v. *New York,** by way of a Frankfurterian deferral in *Poe* v. *Ullman,*[65] to the holding in *Griswold* v. *Connecticut*[66] that a state's anti-birth-control statutes violate a right of privacy derived from "the penumbras" of the First, Third, Fourth, Fifth and Ninth amendments.†

We tell ourselves often that after the Marshall period— which is *sui generis;* it happened, was great, beneficial, not for mere mortals to judge, and is our Greco-Roman period—after the Taney consolidation and moderation, after the ghastly error of *Dred Scott* and the Civil War and all that, came the bad years, the Middle Ages, when men were benighted, and nearly brought the institution to ruin. Wise and rational men, shouting *écraser l'infâme,* saved the Court and set it on the right path. If something

---

* *Lochner* held maximum-hour legislation unconstitutional. See *supra,* p. 21.

† Poe v. Ullman, decided in 1961, concerned the same Connecticut statutes that were held unconstitutional in Griswold v. Connecticut in 1965. But, unlike *Griswold,* Poe v. Ullman was not a criminal prosecution, and at the time it arose, Connecticut had had a long history of not enforcing its anti-birth-control laws. A closely-divided Supreme Court, Justice Frankfurter writing, held in Poe v. Ullman that the Court would not undertake to decide the constitutionality of anti-birth-control statutes which, although unrepealed and in some measure, perhaps, effective, lay dormant and unenforced.

has gone wrong again, it is that the path has been strayed from. But that is not so. The path on which the men of our Enlightenment set the Court is a broad avenue. Visibility is low. Convenient stopping places as well as ultimate destination are uncertain, indeed unknowable. Give or take so many steps from the center line and byways here or there, and allowing, of course, for different modes and rates of marching, it is more nearly true that the Warren Court has traveled the main highway of the institution's history.

Chapter 3

The Web of Subjectivity

The Warren Court has come under professional criticism for erratic subjectivity of judgment, for analytical laxness, for what amounts to intellectual incoherence in many opinions, and for imagining too much history. Whatever precisely may be meant by content analysis, we have not—I guess happily—undertaken enough of it on a systematic basis to have produced a quantitative, let alone qualitative, yardstick with which to determine whether this Court was substantially weaker analytically, less craftsmanlike, more manipulative of its materials, and more subjective than prior Courts that are now held in high esteem.

Perhaps *Marbury* v. *Madison*[1] stands up better analytically than *Reynolds* v. *Sims*[2] and *Wesberry* v. *Sanders*,[3] the main reapportionment cases. Perhaps it is easier to manage an analytical accommodation between John Marshall's decisions in *Gibbons* v. *Ogden*[4] and *Willson* v. *Black Bird Creek Marsh Co.*,[5] than between the Warren Court's decisions, let us say, in *Gray* v. *Sanders*[6] and *Fortson* v. *Morris*.[7] Marshall held that a steamboat monopoly on the Hudson River was an obstruction to commerce forbidden by federal statutes regulating navigation and by the Commerce Clause of the Constitution, but that a dam barring a navigable stream was not such an obstruction. The Warren Court found the Georgia county-unit system unconstitutional because under it a minority of voters could elect a governor, but thought it perfectly constitutional for a still malapportioned Georgia legislature to choose as governor the candidate who had got a smaller share of the popular vote than his opponent. And maybe the White Court was more skillful and more craftsmanlike in its golden years just before World War I, when in Tocqueville's phrase,[8] it steered out of a tide that threatened to carry it away, and sustained some Progressive legislation, while taking care not quite to abandon its principles.

Readers, for example, of the *Pipe Line Cases* of 1914, which upheld federal rate regulation of oil pipelines, did not think well of the White Court's craftsmanship then, and would not do so now.[9] Holmes, who wrote the desperately negotiated opinion in those cases, noted in the margin of his own copy of it that he regarded the reasoning "as inadequate . . . but was compelled to strike out what I thought the real argument," and to his former colleague Moody he said privately that he believed the other judges' "reasons for desiring the omissions were extra-legal—and the result is that I put my name to something that does not satisfy or represent my views. . . . I never was so disturbed but I thought it my duty to let it go as the majority was content."[10] Nor does *Wilson* v. *New*,[11] upholding President Wilson's railroad-strike settlement of 1916, parse well.

But this sort of comparison between the Warren Court and its predecessors really does not matter one way or the other, for intellectual incoherence is not excusable and is no more tolerable because it has occurred before. The charges against the Warren Court can be made out, ir-refutably and amply. It will be useful to substantiate them, with some random examples, and to attempt to categorize them, for while they constitute a single web, the web of subjectivity, it is not a seamless one.

Willful simplification of history, not to say distortion, may be viewed as either the least or the most damaging failure of process, but it is, at any rate, the most fre-quently gratuitous. History is often enough inconclusive, and a Court willing to shoulder the responsibility for judgment, a Court that does not seek to extort from his-tory a crutch for its results, need seldom find in it an impediment to reaching them. Yet, on more than a few occasions, the Warren Court has purported to discover in the history of the Fourteenth Amendment, and of the Thirteenth, and of other constitutional provisions, the crutch that wasn't there.

Thus it is indisputable, as the Court said in *South*

Carolina v. *Katzenbach*,*[12] that Congress is empowered by Section 5 of the Fourteenth Amendment to enact appropriate enforcement legislation. But then, in *Katzenbach* v. *Morgan*,†[13] the Court held that Section 5 is a plenary grant of legislative power, enabling Congress, not only to implement, but to supplement the guarantees of the Fourteenth Amendment, without regard to limitations under which the Amendment operates when applied of its own force.[14] Conceivably this pronouncement wisely enlarges national legislative power and wisely reallocates functions between Court and Congress,[15] but history it is not.

The Framers of the Fourteenth Amendment explicitly rejected the option of an open-ended grant of power to Congress freely to meddle with conditions within the states, so as to render them equal in accordance with Congress's own notions. Rather, federal power, legislative as well as judicial, was to be limited by the terms of the Amendment. The Court's distortion of the history of the matter became transparent in a footnote in which the Court added that Section 5 was to be read as enabling

* In this case, the Court upheld the constitutionality in general of the Voting Rights Act of 1965, as applied to prevent continued discrimination against Negro voters in certain Southern states. The Act, among other provisions, forbids use of literacy tests in those states, and authorizes the Attorney General to undertake the registration of voters with federal personnel. See *infra*, p. 58.

† The *Morgan* case concerned a special provision of the Voting Rights Act, which enfranchised Puerto Ricans literate in Spanish only, even though the state law in New York, where the case arose, establishes literacy in English as a qualification for voting. The Court held this provision of the Voting Rights Act also constitutional.

Congress to enlarge on the terms of the Fourteenth Amendment, but not "to exercise discretion in the other direction" by diluting or restricting them. It was precisely because they feared both enlargement and dilution, and because they saw legislative power to do either as necessarily importing power to do the other, that the Framers builded as they built, and not as the Court said they built.

A couple of years after *Katzenbach* v. *Morgan*, the Court found another avenue to the same end of enhancing Congressional power to deal with problems of racial discrimination. Again the Court's reliance was in history. The Court held in *Jones* v. *Mayer Co.*,[16] in 1968, that the Civil Rights Act of 1866, which was enacted to implement the Thirteenth Amendment, was intended to forbid private racial discrimination in real-estate transactions, and that the Thirteenth Amendment empowers Congress to legislate against such private discriminations because they constitute a badge of the slavery the Amendment abolished. (The Fourteenth Amendment, except as the Court presented it to Congress in rather refurbished form in *Katzenbach* v. *Morgan*, proscribes only discrimination by government or under government auspices, not private discrimination.)

Perhaps the Court's reading of history is not in this instance, as Justice Harlan said in dissent, "almost surely wrong," but the answer yielded by the historical materials is infinitely more complex and dubious than the Court made it out to be.[17] And in *Miranda* v. *Arizona*, in which, instituting a radical, if justifiable, departure from prior practice, the Court extended the right to counsel from the courtroom to the stationhouse, it decorated its opinion

49

with a brief historical exercise aimed at proving the unprovable, namely, that the reform the Court was now launching was but "an application of principles long recognized and applied in other settings."[18]

More serious—in one sense only—than these misadventures with history are instances of *ad hoc* subjectivity resulting in palpable injustice to individuals. In an unbroken course of decision from 1957 to 1966, as Dean C. Peter Magrath has observed, the Supreme Court seemed to confirm a prediction of Professor Harry Kalven, Jr., that the concept of obscenity would come to be restricted "to something akin to hard-core pornography. To be sure, no one could define it, but all intelligent men could instantly recognize it. In no decision after 1957 did the Court uphold a finding of obscenity. In twelve cases it overturned judgments against nearly two hundred items ranging from such serious works as Henry Miller's *Tropic of Cancer* to such potboilers as *Trailer Trollop* and *The Wife-Swappers*."[19]

The Justices rested decision on many grounds, often, in numerous *per curiam* orders, on none, and they could hardly be said to be following an intelligible and communicable principle of decision. Yet, by 1966, a rule had emerged whose effect, at least, was intelligible. In March of that year, however, while holding that *Fanny Hill* had redeeming social value and could not be suppressed, the Court affirmed the obscenity convictions of one Edward Mishkin, a purveyor of sado-masochistic and homosexual pulp, and of Ralph Ginzburg, publisher of *Liaison*, a biweekly newsletter concerned with sex; *Eros*, a hard-cover magazine devoted in part to fairly explicit descriptions of sexual activities; and *The Housewife's Handbook of Selective Promiscuity,* which also contained detailed descriptions of sexual encounters.[20]

The vagaries of the subjective individual judgments that the Justices were pressing into service as the law of the Constitution merely caused intellectual anguish to professional observers of the Court, but they fell rather hard on the Messrs. Mishkin and Ginzburg, who were subject, respectively, to three- and five-year prison sentences, not to speak of heavy fines. The *Ginzburg* conviction particularly was a grim episode in the temple of justice. For, though the process would remain subjective nevertheless, one might succeed in distinguishing Mishkin's case, and also *Fanny Hill.* Mishkin's wares could conceivably fall within a zone in which lower courts were entitled to classify them as hard-core pornography, or else, in terms of the Court's purported test, they could be deemed to be patently offensive, to have prurient appeal, and to lack social value—and hence to be obscene.

I do not mean that, viewed in this light, the *Mishkin* case is free from difficulties; merely that *Ginzburg* is fraught with greater ones. *Fanny Hill,* for its, or her, part, is old pornography; its style is eighteenth-century, it is of historical interest, and might on this score qualify as having what the Court calls redeeming social value. But what was the difference—any imaginable difference—between Ginzburg's books and magazines and the many items the Court had tolerated in the years before, including, in addition to those already mentioned, *Pleasure Was My Business,* describing abnormal exercises in a Florida brothel, *MANual* and *Grecian Guild Pictorial,* and the film

51

A Stranger Knocks, in which there is a scene that even the least worldly must interpret as representing sexual intercourse?[21]

Against this background, the only sense one could make of the *Ginzburg* case was that it marked a concerted, collective change of attitude, a hardening of attitude. The subjective judgments of a majority of the Justices would thenceforth be more restrictive than they had been. The judgments would remain subjective and difficult to predict, but there was a new threshold, and it was higher. This much we had been vouchsafed, and Mr. Ginzburg was the megaphone through which the Court made its announcement.

In common with virtually all observers, Mr. Ginzburg had thought when, in 1961, he commenced publication of his *Eros,* "the magazine of sexual candor," that the venture was made possible by "recent court decisions that have realistically interpreted America's obscenity laws and that have given to this country a new breath of freedom of expression."[22] A lay opinion only, to be sure, but one thoroughly grounded in the expectations of more qualified observers. In 1966, the Supreme Court defeated these expectations, and a bitter lesson that was for Mr. Ginzburg. Nevertheless, the defeat of such expectations is often unavoidable, if our system of case law is to be flexible and vital. Law that is made in cases is commonly retroactive, and in order to change and grow it must sometimes defeat expectations. But then in May of the following year, in three cases, one each from New York, Kentucky, and Arkansas, the Supreme Court, writing the briefest kind of *per curiam* opinion, held that two paperbacks, *Lustpool* and *Shame Agent*, and a series of girlie magazines, *High Heels, Spree, Gent, Swank, Bachelor, Modern Man, Cavalcade, Gentlemen, Ace,* and *Sir,* were not obscene.*[23]

Now these publications are no more distinguishable from Ginzburg's than were all those items that went before, from 1957 to 1966. *Lustpool* and *Shame Agent*, for example, were characterized in District Attorney Frank Hogan's brief as describing in detail a male protagonist's "sexual encounters—both natural and perverse—with numerous females, including in at least one instance, two females at the same time." So it appeared, and has continued to appear since, that the Court changed its attitude back again, simply leap-frogging Mr. Ginzburg. There is no new threshold after all, or if there was, it was there for Ginzburg alone and no one else to trip over.

The only effort, so called, to differentiate Ginzburg's case in the short order in which the Court announced its decision of May, 1967, was the remark that there was no evidence this time "of the sort of 'pandering' which the Court found significant in *Ginzburg* v. *United States.*" The pandering notion was based on Ginzburg's advertising, which, one hastens to say, was lucid, but nowhere near as explicit as the product it sold. The notion has its difficulties. Passing them, however, it is impossible to see how publications titled *Lustpool* and *Shame Agent*, or those girlie magazines, with the pictures and blurbs that

---

* The Court does allow states to prevent circulation of materials such as these to juveniles. See Ginsberg v. New York, 390 U.S. 629 (1968); but cf. Interstate Circuit, Inc. v. Dallas, 390 U.S. 676 (1968), and Rabeck v. New York, 391 U.S. 462 (1968).

adorn them, all held not obscene in May, 1967, could be said to pander any less than Ginzburg's advertising.

What happened to Ralph Ginzburg was not one of those regrettable but unavoidable vicissitudes encountered in the retroactive development of case law. It was not even a failure by the Court to review and overturn a lower-court judgment. Such a failure to review, as by a denial of certiorari, might be explained as an oversight, or attributed to institutional administrative needs, and would be unfortunate, but again, a cost that sometimes must be borne for having a Supreme Court at all. Or a failure to review may be explained by the peculiar doctrinal difficulty or dilemma presented in a case, or by its political sensitivity. The injustice then would be nearly equally intolerable if—but only if—the judgment that the Court allowed to stand was inconsistent with applicable prior decisions of the Court, and as hard on the individual as Ginzburg's prison sentence was on him.[24]

Even so, there is a difference between withholding law or judgment, and making both capriciously and unequally. In the *Ginzburg* case, the Court punished a man under a rule applicable to no one else, past or future. It made of Mr. Ginzburg an example that exemplified nothing. Had any other institution been responsible for this performance—say some hapless administrative agency—the Court would have been well justified in finding a violation of the Due Process and Equal Protection Clauses.

Although the problem is more complex, one may regard as almost equally shocking the manner in which the Court limited the retroactive effect of a number of its decisions in matters of criminal procedure, notably *Miranda* v. *Ari-*

zona.[25] (*Miranda* held that police interrogation of a suspect to whom a lawyer has not been made available is in most circumstances unconstitutional.)

In other recent criminal cases, the Warren Court sometimes applied new rules of criminal procedure retroactively, and sometimes not. It worked out certain distinctions to explain the difference, and then it promptly blurred them.[26] But when it denied retroactive application to a new rule, the Court did so with respect to judgments of conviction that had become final; judgments, this is to say, that under generally applicable standards governing appealability could no longer be reviewed on appeal or certiorari. Nevertheless, being criminal, such judgments remain open to collateral attack by means of a petition for a writ of habeas corpus. For obvious practical reasons, the process of decision and review must stop sometime—reasons of the economy of judicial effort, if no other ones, so dictate in all areas of litigation—but the writ of habeas corpus does make collateral review of criminal convictions available without limit of time. Hence the distinction between convictions that could still be reviewed directly on appeal or certiorari and convictions that had become final was not an entirely satisfactory one. Yet it was more satisfactory than the altogether arbitrary distinction the Court began to take, starting in 1966, with respect to *Miranda* and a number of other decisions, including the decisions that counsel should be available at line-ups for identification, and that wire-tap evidence is not admissible in state or federal trials.[27] The distinction the Court now drew was between the cases in which the new rules were actually announced and all other cases, no matter how exactly alike, even if they had already been appealed and were on the Court's docket for decision. At the time of *Miranda* there were a few dozen such other indistinguishable cases pending in the Supreme Court, and the Court refused to disturb the convictions in them.[28]

The injustice is plain, yet the Court gave no reason remotely strong enough to overcome the natural aversion that the judges certainly also felt at such a result. Having concluded that full retroactivity was unwise, presumably because of the risk of a general jail delivery, why did the Court not limit retroactivity, as in the earlier cases, to judgments that were still directly appealable? To be sure, prosecutors and trial judges had relied on the prior, now superseded, rules of procedure, but that was true as well in cases in which new rules were applied retroactively to judgments not yet final. The new rules concerning the right to counsel were not aimed only at improving the fact-finding process at trial, and the Court did not necessarily suppose that any conviction obtained in violation of them put into question that process and the guilt of the accused. The rules rested in substantial part on more general considerations of the fairness and efficacy of the administration of criminal justice; and that was entirely true of the decisions concerning admissibility of wire-tap evidence. But it was entirely true as well of an earlier decision concerning the admissibility of illegally seized evidence, and yet that decision had been applied retroactively to judgments not yet final, even if only to such judgments. The *Miranda* decision, and most particularly the line-up identification decision, which were not so applied, rested in greater part, if in part only, on considerations having to do with the reliability of the basic fact-finding process.

There was a way to avoid the blatant injustice, which the Court in fact committed, of applying new rules only to a random few lucky defendants in whose cases they were announced. The Court could have made its new rules altogether prospective, not applying them even to the defendants in the cases before it; in other words, it could have decided these cases under previously applicable rules, and given notice that it had fashioned new rules for the future, to be applied to trials commencing after a date certain. Except for reversing the convictions of one or two lucky parties, that was what the Court was doing anyway. It might simply have omitted the lucky ones also.

Briefly, in a sentence, the Court indicated its view that "[s]ound policies of decision-making, rooted in the command of Article III of the Constitution that we resolve issues solely in concrete cases or controversies, and in the possible effect upon the incentive of counsel to advance contentions requiring a change in the law," militate against use of this technique.[29] But a couple of years before, in its first decision limiting retroactivity to cases in which judgments had not yet become final, the Court had suggested that it would be free to announce rules for future application only.[30] And in any event, unless it thought it was constitutionally foreclosed from taking this avenue, which it did not quite say, should the Court not at least have engaged in some weighing of the shortcomings of pure prospectivity, as against the arbitrariness of the disposition it was making?

In such a case as *Ginzburg,* and after an attenuated

57

fashion, somewhat more understandably, in the retroactivity decisions, there was a breakdown of process, and of elementary justice. There are other, more numerous instances of the failure of process, but not necessarily of individual justice. Among these, the most readily identifiable are cases in which the Court stamps its foot, as it were, and refuses to enter into argument on a, or the, decisive issue. The Warren Court inaugurated this practice—for itself; it is not wholly unprecedented—early in its career, as for example when it made the transition by *per curiam* order from *Brown* v. *Board of Education* to cases of segregation in other public facilities, and when it shook off in two or three assertive sentences a major question concerning the federal treaty power.[31] A great many of the obscenity cases fall into the foot-stamping category, whatever else may be said of them, most especially the post-*Ginzburg* opinion of May, 1967, concerning *Lustpool, Shame Agent,* and all those girlie magazines.

The Warren Court seemed particularly prone to spare itself the travail of argument in cases touching the basic rules that define its own jurisdiction. A partial explanation, but not an excuse, is that the parties, with the ineffable optimism of litigants, often fail to press such issues; both sides are anxious to have the Court decide. Thus in *South Carolina* v. *Katzenbach*, which held the Voting Rights Act of 1965 constitutional, the Court needed to determine, before it could go on to other matters, whether the moving party, the State of South Carolina, had standing to bring the lawsuit. This is an issue with a past and with a future, with implications and ramifications. The passage in which the Court disposed of it reads, in its entirety, as follows: "Original jurisdiction is founded on the presence of a controversy between a State and a citizen of another State under Art. III, §. 2 of the Constitution"—followed by the citation of a case that, if not altogether inapposite, was certainly not dispositive.[32]

A more elaborate example of the same phenomenon is *Harper* v. *Virginia Board of Elections*,[33] declaring the poll tax unconstitutional. The poll tax, said the Court, is not plausibly related to "any legitimate state interest in the conduct of elections." But "the Court gives no reason," complained Justice Black in dissent, and it did not. Also dissenting, Justice Harlan argued that payment of a minimal poll tax might very well be thought to promote "civic responsibility, weeding out those who do not care enough about public affairs to pay one dollar and fifty cents or thereabouts a year for the exercise of the franchise." The Court failed even to address itself to this aspect of the issue, simply asserting that "payment of a fee as a measure of a voter's qualifications" was "a capricious or irrelevant factor." An unworthy factor, quite possibly, ugly, petty, mean, but as Justice Harlan had just demonstrated, not necessarily capricious or irrelevant.

The Court touched on, but did not adopt, a quite different justification for its result. It quoted Judge Thornberry, of a three-judge lower court that had struck down the Texas poll tax in another case, as remarking that if Texas were to place a tax, however small and reasonable, on the right to speak, no court would hesitate to declare it unconstitutional, for such a tax would violate the First and Fourteenth Amendments. There is difficulty with this ground of decision, since, as Mr. Justice Black suggested, the right to speak could also not be freely abridged on the basis of age, illiteracy, conviction of a felony, or residence; and yet the right to vote is commonly qualified on these grounds. Nevertheless, the result in *Harper* could more easily have been supported by assimilating the right to vote to First Amendment rights, although there is history, and there are other considerations, to overcome. The Court, at any rate, did not take this course. The opinion it wrote seemed to Professor Archibald Cox—a former Solicitor General, and a friendly critic surely; indeed, as he himself allows, an affectionately sympathetic one—"almost perversely to repudiate every conventional guide to legal judgment," except as it relied, somewhat inscrutably, Mr. Cox may agree, on the one-man, one-vote reapportionment decisions.[34]

The poll-tax case may be seen in another light, more indulgently, perhaps. It confronted the Court with the problem of line drawing, which is central to the task of judging, as Professor Louis Henkin has reminded us,[35] and unavoidable certainly by judges not totally addicted to absolutes. *Harper* v. *Virginia Board of Elections* is not alone in exhibiting a tendency to nationalize and level standards of qualification for voting, as we shall presently.[36] This is the tendency that is immanent in references to the one-person, one-vote apportionment rule. It could be brought to fruition by assimilating the right to vote to First Amendment rights. But the Court hesitated to go that far.

The alternative to adoption of a far-reaching principle is line drawing, judgment of and by degree. Yet the judgment of degree may be impossible to make save by sheer arbitrariness, and then the judge's only remaining choice is to sacrifice the result he would like to reach, the result that conforms to the tendency he favors but is not quite willing to follow to its principled conclusion. This choice the Warren Court, all too often, would not accept. So in *Harper* it did not pay the price of its hesitancy to nationalize and level qualifications for voting, but insisted on a conclusion that it did not bother to reason through, because it will not wash.

The invincible impulse to have the cake and eat it, or, in another festive figure, to dance but not pay the piper, may be observed also in *Katzenbach* v. *Morgan*,[37] sustaining Section 4(e) of the Voting Rights Act of 1965, which enfranchises Puerto Ricans literate in Spanish only, and thus overrides the requirement of the law of New York of literacy in English. One branch of the Court's holding proceeded from a distortion of historical materials.* Another ground of decision was that even if, in the absence of a showing that the vote is denied on the basis of race, Congress has no direct power to change the electoral law of New York, Congress does have power to cure or forestall other discriminations practiced by the state in violation of the Fourteenth Amendment. Therefore, the Court argued, if Congress thought that Puerto Ricans might otherwise be discriminated against by law or administrative action in New York, it had the power to enfranchise them as a means of preventing such other discrimination, on the theory that the vote would enable them better to protect themselves. Instead of directly at-

* See *supra*, pp. 48–49.

tacking official discrimination practiced against Puerto Ricans, this is to say, as it plainly could have done under the Fourteenth Amendment, Congress decided to reach it indirectly, by securing the vote for the Puerto Ricans. The vote is thus seen as a means of enforcing the Fourteenth Amendment, not as itself the end of the Congressional action, and the problem of whether Congress has plenary power to set qualifications for voting is avoided.

The Court could adduce not a shred of evidence that Puerto Ricans are indeed discriminated against by state action in New York, but perhaps with some stretching the presumption of constitutionality might fill the gap. The stretching would be considerable; all the way from a presumption buttressed by data, even if data "offered not for the truth of the facts asserted but only to establish that responsible persons have made the assertions and hold the opinions which are disclosed,"[38] to a presumption that makes up for the lack of any data at all—a presumption that, in a case such as this, puts the party attacking constitutionality to the task of proving a negative. Be that as it may, the difficulty is that any group which does not have the vote in New York—aliens, citizens of New Jersey, twenty-year-olds—may be thought to be in danger of being discriminated against in other ways as well; certainly there is at least as much evidence that New York discriminates against aliens and against citizens of New Jersey as there is that it discriminates against Puerto Ricans. Consequently, if the Court's reasoning is taken seriously, Congress could bestow the vote on these groups, and on any group which it fears may be discriminated against, even though its fears are grounded solely in the fact that the group in question is deprived of the vote.

There is then nothing left of any constraint on the power of Congress to set qualifications for voting in state elections. Yet the Court did not purport to vest plenary power in Congress. The Court's ground of decision proved too much, and yet the Court purported to place a limited decision on it. Nor was the Court prepared to take the analytically coherent—if otherwise questionable—position that a requirement of literacy in English, or of literacy at all, is an unjustifiable impediment to the right to vote, any more than in the poll-tax case it was willing to assimilate the right to vote to First Amendment rights. Nor, again, did it choose to rest decision on an alternate ground, adopted by a lower court, which drew Congressional authority from the power to govern territories such as Puerto Rico, and to protect citizens of those territories when they move to the mainland. There are analytical difficulties here also, but one may think lesser ones.[39]

In *Flast* v. *Cohen*,[40] the Court held that a federal taxpayer, *qua* taxpayer, has standing to bring suit attacking a federal expenditure on the ground that it violates the Establishment of Religion Clause of the First Amendment. It had previously been held, and long understood, that being a federal taxpayer did not alone entitle one to come into a federal court and challenge the validity of a federal expenditure, or of any other federal action, except if the challenge went to the tax itself, or if a tax was earmarked to an expenditure.[41]

The issue may be of constitutional dimensions, although the Court did not so treat it, but in any event the

Justices were not ready simply to open the courts to federal taxpayers, as such, and in general. Yet, again, they were unwilling also to accept the cost of their hesitancy. So they held that a taxpayer will be allowed to litigate only the constitutionality of a federal spending program, not "an incidental expenditure of tax funds in the administration of an essentially regulatory statute," and then only when he attacks spending that "exceeds specific constitutional limitations imposed upon the exercise of the Congressional taxing and spending power," and not "simply" an expenditure that is claimed to be "generally beyond the powers delegated to Congress."

At the very earliest impact of analysis, the question that this holding raises is, what in the world does it mean? The Establishment Clause, which the taxpayer in *Flast* v. *Cohen* was allowed to invoke, is not any sort of specific limitation on spending, and it is certainly also an equally "specific" limitation on the exercise of other powers, if "specific" at all. And if the Establishment Clause is read as a specific limitation on spending, in what sense are other provisions of the Constitution, including the Fourteenth Amendment, and including the Tenth, which was involved in the principal earlier case that denied standing to a taxpayer, a case the Court now purported not to be overruling[42]—in what sense are these provisions not equally limitations on spending?[43]

Taxpayers in recent years have brought suit, *qua* taxpayers, challenging the authority of Federal Reserve Banks under the Federal Reserve Act of 1913 to issue notes as currency, on the ground of inconsistency with the clause in Article I, Section 8 of the Constitution empowering Congress to coin money and regulate its value; and challenging issuance by the Postmaster General of a commemorative Christmas stamp showing the Madonna, on the ground that the action violated the Establishment Clause.[44] Under the holding in *Flast* v. *Cohen,* may these suits be maintained, and if not, why not?

It isn't that these apparently insufferable line-drawing dilemmas are always thrust upon the Court. Presumably the Court could not very well, or could not long, avoid passing on the constitutionality of Section 4(e) of the Voting Rights Act of 1965, and perhaps, although the presumption is a good bit weaker, it could not much longer allow litigation to mount posing the question whether taxpayers could bring suit under the Establishment Clause. But the Court quite gratuitously reached out for a similar dilemma in *Reitman* v. *Mulkey.*[45]

By vote of the people, in November, 1964, California adopted a constitutional amendment—called Proposition 14—prohibiting tLe state, or any of its subdivisions or agencies, directly or indirectly to limit or abridge the right of any person to sell or rent, or decline to sell or rent, his real property to anyone he chose, "in his absolute discretion." Proposition 14 repealed fair-housing laws then on the books in California. In an obscure opinion, the California Supreme Court held Proposition 14 invalid as a violation of the Fourteenth Amendment to the United States Constitution. This might seem well enough, but the Supreme Court of the United States did not let it alone. It brought the case up by granting certiorari, and it then shied away from deciding it on the basis of an ultimate principle, namely, that with respect to housing, or at least some forms of housing (*e.g.*, tax-exempt, or publicly-aided in other ways), the state cannot be neutral, and the Fourteenth Amendment's prohibition of discriminatory state action means that the state has an affirmative duty to prevent, or seek to prevent, discrimination.[46]

My colleague Charles L. Black, Jr., has argued power-fully—as persuasively as possible—that a coherent narrower rationale was available. California, after all, reverted to a position of neutrality, neither supporting nor forbidding discrimination in housing, if that is what California did, not simply by repealing a statute, but by a constitutional amendment that disabled all organs of government from legislating against discrimination. For a group assumed to be largely racially defined, California thus imposed an obstacle on the route to obtaining desired government action which does not normally stand in the way for other groups wishing "to use political processes to get what they want." Negroes in California who wanted fair-housing leg-islation locally or statewide now had to travel the arduous road of constitutional amendment.[47] They were thus sub-jected to discrimination on account of their race, no less so than if some other form of political disability had been visited on them.

The initial difficulty with this line of argument is that Mr. Black treats Proposition 14 as if it said that no law or ordinance shall be enacted limiting the right of any per-son to decline to sell or rent his property to a Negro. But Proposition 14 does not say that, and it is not so clear in practice that only Negroes are discriminated against in real-estate transactions in California, or that Negroes were the only group seeking the enactment of anti-discrimination laws.⁴⁸ It cannot be that California has quite rid herself of religious, ethnic, social, and miscellaneous housing discriminations.

In *Hunter* v. *Erickson*, a year and a half after *Reitman* v. *Mulkey*, the Court, adopting Mr. Black's theory, held invalid an amendment to the Akron, Ohio, city charter, which required approval by a majority of the electorate in a referendum of any ordinance seeking to regulate the sale or lease of real property "on the basis of race, color, religion, national origin or ancestry." Said the Court: "Here, unlike *Reitman,* there was an explicitly racial classification treating racial housing matters differently from other racial and housing matters. . . . The automatic referendum system does not reach housing discrimination on sexual or political grounds, or against those with children or dogs."⁴⁹ Unlike *Reitman!*

Aside from the problem of identifying a racial classification in *Reitman* v. *Mulkey,* Mr. Black's theory of the decision, adopted by the Court for purposes of *Hunter* v. *Erickson,* raises other questions. What of a state constitutional amendment, such as New York's Blaine Amendment,⁵⁰ forbidding state aid to parochial schools of the sort that only or chiefly Catholics are interested in, and going in its prohibition well beyond the First Amendment of the United States Constitution; that is, a state constitutional amendment denying to Catholic schools (without specifically naming them, of course) state aid that the federal Constitution would permit them to have, and yet again not going so far in the direction of disestablishment as to infringe the freedom of religious exercise?

Mr. Black suggests, very consistently, that if such a

state constitutional provision would also fall under his theory, then for his part, so be it. But others might find this result troublesome. After all, any constitutional amendment or other special law-making procedure, such as a referendum or a two-thirds voting requirement in the legislature, amounts to giving minorities a measure of veto power; to put it another way, such devices represent a decision to do some things only by majorities greater—or harder to obtain—than the usual ones, because, it may be thought, some things cannot be done effectively unless action is based on a particularly broad consensus. How much leeway to seek a desired broad consensus would Mr. Black's interpretation of *Reitman* v. *Mulkey*, and the Court's own subsequent decision in *Hunter* v. *Erickson*, leave a state or municipality?

A federal district judge in Milwaukee, in part because he was persuaded by Mr. Black's argument, enjoined the city council from adopting, or referring for vote by the entire city electorate, a resolution that the council shall not enact any ordinance restricting the rights of owners of real estate to sell, lease, or rent private property. Such a resolution, the court assumed, could be binding on the council for two years.[51] Another federal court has held that it was permissible simply to submit a fair-housing statute to a referendum.[52] In Toledo, Ohio, a fair-housing ordinance was repealed by referendum, and the effect there may be that future fair-housing ordinances can no longer be enacted by the city council, but must abide another vote of the people. Under the decision in *Hunter* v. *Erickson*, presumably the repeal is unconstitutional if the ordinance can be classified as dealing explicitly with racial discrimination. Yet the Supreme Court declined to hear the Toledo case, probably because it was not clear on the record to what extent the repeal by referendum does in fact prevent future action by the city council.[53]

With some forcing of the facts, and not without undertaking an inquiry into legislative motives which, for good reason, it normally shuns,[54] the Court might have disposed of *Reitman* v. *Mulkey* by holding that in the specific circumstances of California in 1964, Proposition 14 did not put the state in any sort of neutral position, but constituted an affirmative encouragement of racial discrimination,[55] just as in the peculiar circumstances of Prince Edward County, Virginia, in 1959, the closing of the public schools there was viewed not as a withdrawal of the state from the field of education, but as an effort to sustain a policy of school segregation.[56] But the Court in *Reitman* v. *Mulkey* took neither this route to decision nor Mr. Black's; it took, in truth, no route. Professors Kenneth Karst and Harold Horowitz, than whom the Warren Court had no more compassionate critics, concluded that the Court's several line-drawing efforts came to "no satisfactory doctrinal explanation for the result in *Reitman* v. *Mulkey*. Just when the reader thinks he is about to discover the ground for decision, the opinion moves on to discuss something else, leaving the earlier point dangling."[57]

Not quite sure of the true direction of progress, but unwilling to pay the price of its uncertainty, the Court in these cases floundered. Messrs. Karst and Horowitz very perspicaciously lead into their article on *Reitman* v. *Mulkey* by quoting from the reminiscences of Felix Frankfurter a passage telling of T. R. Powell's outrage at Holmes's ill-reasoned opinion in the *Pipe Line Cases.*＊ Just so. The performance of the White Court in the years from 1911 to 1917 is almost precisely apposite. The only difference is that the White Court was very clear indeed about the direction that the progress of legislation was taking. What it was unwilling to do was to abandon its own principles and go along fully. But it floundered in much the same fashion. Yet as Messrs. Karst and Horowitz do not fail to recall, Frankfurter chided Powell and bade him remember that "the important point [in the *Pipe Line Cases*] was to get an adjudication which would sustain the statute. The vital fact is that the statute was sustained."[58]

A valiant but unavailing attempt by the Warren Court to do better than flounder is *Witherspoon* v. *Illinois,* which it is instructive to contrast with *United States* v. *Jackson,* decided by the Court two months before *Witherspoon.* Both cases concerned the death penalty and the manner of its imposition. In both, particularly in *Witherspoon,* it was clear that a majority of the Warren Court disfavored capital punishment, as well it might, and that it was aware of a movement for abolition which is manifesting itself in various guises throughout the country, and of a body of litigation aimed at enlisting the Court in support of the movement, if not at making it the instrument of the movement's success.[59]

The Warren Court's sensitivity to these trends in itself contrasted markedly with the Vinson Court's hasty co-

＊ See *supra,* pp. 46–47.

operation in the execution of Julius and Ethel Rosenberg. It was clear as well, again particularly in *Witherspoon,* that the Warren Court took quite seriously the argument that the death penalty is unconstitutional as a cruel and unusual punishment, in violation of the Eighth Amendment; it may not be too much to say that several of the Justices had at least tentatively identified this as the true line of progress.[60] Yet a majority was also at the moment not prepared to go this far. Nevertheless, in *Witherspoon,* beguiled by an insufficient analysis, the Court refused to bear the cost.

Like a great many states, Illinois allows but does not require the jury in murder cases to impose the death penalty. And again like a great many states, Illinois permits the prosecution to challenge and exclude from the jury in a capital case jurors who have "conscientious scruples against capital punishment," or are "opposed to the same." Not only persons, therefore, who declare that under no circumstances would they impose capital punishment, and who thus in a sense prejudge the case, but prospective jurors who admit to scruples but do not feel that they would invariably be compelled to vote against capital punishment are excluded from juries, and were excluded in the *Witherspoon* case.

The Court was invited to hold that juries so constituted are necessarily prosecution-minded, and cannot impartially determine the very question of guilt itself. But the Court found the sociological evidence offered to support the hypothesis that persons who have no scruples against the death penalty would in general tend to favor the prosecution's point of view too fragmentary and uncer-

71

tain, and hence it did not rest its decision on this ground, and did not reverse Witherspoon's conviction of murder. The Court held rather that the Illinois legislature had charged the jury to "express the conscience of the community on the ultimate question of life or death," and that "a jury composed exclusively [of people without conscientious scruples about the death penalty] cannot speak for the community," which in Illinois as elsewhere, according to public-opinion polls anyway, includes many persons who object to capital punishment. A state, the Court held, may exclude prospective jurors who have prejudged the case, in effect, because they are unwilling under any circumstances to impose the death penalty. "But when it swept from the jury all who expressed conscientious or religious scruples against capital punishment and all who opposed it in principle," said the Court, "the State crossed the line of neutrality. In its quest for a jury capable of imposing the death penalty, the state produced a jury uncommonly willing to condemn men to die." And the Court concluded: "Whatever else might be said of capital punishment, it is at least clear that its imposition by a hanging jury cannot be squared with the Constitution. The state of Illinois has stacked the deck against the petitioner."

This is all very attractive, and certainly in the present evolving state of public and judicial opinion the Court should not have legitimated a death sentence by affirming it, thus lending its prestige to the remaining forces that favor continuation of capital punishment. But, like *Reitman* v. *Mulkey*, the *Witherspoon* case had been taken in the Court's discretionary certiorari jurisdiction. It need not have been brought up for decision. Or else the Court might have disposed of it by holding that legislatures may not leave imposition of the death penalty to the discretion of the jury without laying down standards governing the exercise of that discretion.

The trouble with the Court's actual decision is that it does not meet a crucial point made by Mr. Justice White, speaking for himself in dissent. The Court did not deny that the legislature could itself decree a particular automatic penalty, including death, for all defendants convicted of a given crime, thus leaving no discretion to judge or jury. The legislature cannot dispense with the function of judge and jury in determining guilt. It would obviously lack due process for a legislature to decree that an individual was guilty of a crime. But the argument cuts, if at all, rather the other way when it comes to the choice of sanctions. The decision whether or not the death penalty, and perhaps other grave sanctions, should be imposed is one that ought arguably to be made by the highest and most responsible organs of the state. It ought not to be simply delegable to judges or juries, at least not without standards, not without a general indication from the legislature of the considerations that must govern the exercise of the jury's or the judge's discretion. But if legislatures are free to decide when the death penalty is to be imposed, asked Justice White, if, he might have added, it is, indeed, preferable that legislatures make the decision, and yet delegation to juries is allowed, why should legislatures be "disabled from delegating the penalty decision to a group who will impose the death penalty more often than would a group differently chosen?"

All the answer the Court offered to this question, in a footnote at that, was that Illinois had not undertaken to fix the death penalty by legislation, but had left its imposition to the discretion of a jury, and one of the most important functions of the jury is to maintain a link between community values and the penal system. But that is no answer, because on Mr. Justice White's view, which precisely fits the situation, Illinois had expressed a community value through its legislature. It had said that the death penalty was somewhat preferred, and that the decision whether or not to impose it should be made by citizens who were unsqueamish about it. The Court was not holding that Illinois is required to use a jury as a link between community values and the penal system, and may not use the legislature to make the connection.

Apparently conscious of this missing link in its argument, the Court added that unless the jury is used to translate contemporary community values into penal policy, evolving standards of decency marking the progress of a maturing society could hardly be reflected in the determination of punishment—citing a plurality opinion by Chief Justice Warren in an earlier case, in which the Chief Justice and three other Justices expressed the view that forfeiture of citizenship, if conceived as a punishment, was an unconstitutionally cruel and unusual one.[61] This hint is the beginning, but only the beginning, of quite another argument, namely, that for reasons drawn from the Eighth Amendment, the death penalty cannot be imposed legislatively, in wholesale fashion in a given class of cases, but must be remitted to the discretion of a jury which can more sensitively express a community's standards of decency, from time to time, case by case. This argument, if accepted, would indeed answer Justice White's point. It would turn it around. But the Court did not accept it. It did not even make it.[62]

Justice White's small, still voice of reason remained, thus, unstilled and unanswered. The Court was in a happier position in *United States* v. *Jackson*,[63] where it held unconstitutional a portion of the federal Kidnapping Act which allowed a jury, but not the judge, to impose the death penalty if the kidnapped person had not been freed unharmed. The fault in the provision, the Court held, was that it forced on defendants a choice which discouraged them from exercising their rights to trial by jury. By asking for a jury trial, a defendant put his life in hazard. The provision thus operated as an inducement to waive jury trial. Yet jury trial is a constitutional right, and the choice to exercise it ought to be free.

If the objection to the decision in the *Jackson* case is that the same reasoning would apply to noncapital cases in which a defendant realistically perceived any advantage in pleading guilty or asking for trial before a judge, the answer is that the Court might well extend its reasoning to such cases, or that it need not, or at least need not now decide whether it would, since the threat of the death penalty is something distinct from any other calculus of risks and advantages.[64]

The *Witherspoon* and *Jackson* cases between them, then, serve to mark off the analytically tenable distinction from the arbitrary one. The former sets aside a situation in which a fresh—perhaps only slightly variant, but fresh—choice of values will be called for. The arbitrary distinction separates like from like. Discouraging a man from claiming his right to a jury trial by holding over him the threat of capital punishment is—or at least can be— different from discouraging him in some lesser way, and for some definite and perhaps defensible purpose. But letting a legislature either set the death penalty itself or delegate its imposition to a jury is not different, on the only principles the Court professed to be applying in *Witherspoon*, from letting the legislature delegate the task to a jury least likely to be squeamish.

By the same token, the objection to the poll-tax case is not that the Court was potentially inconsistent in wiping out a disadvantage caused by poverty in one area, when it would plainly not do so in others. Not letting the poor vote is different from not letting the poor take dinner at Le Pavillon, or even not letting them drive because they can't afford a driver's license. The difficulty in the *Harper* case was that the Court chose to characterize imposition of a monetary qualification on the right to vote as capricious, and yet would not meet an argument demonstrating that it was not necessarily capricious.

In *Flast* v. *Cohen* and in *Katzenbach* v. *Morgan*, the trouble was that the Court's ground of decision purported to be limited, but was in truth not limitable. For jurisdictional purposes, taxpayers invoking the Establishment Clause are not distinguishable, except by an arbitrary *ipse dixit*, from other taxpayers attacking federal expenditures on other grounds, and the possibility of discrimination by a state against an identifiable ethnic or racial group which does not vote is not, as a possibility arising from votelessness, to be distinguished from that of discrimination by a state against any other identifiable group lacking the vote.

How the Court, in analytically tenable fashion, isolates occasions for discrete value judgments may be illustrated by a class of free-speech cases. The judgments here are made on thinly distinguishable sets of facts; they are often narrow to the point of being virtually *ad hoc*. Yet though they may be deemed good or bad, wise or unwise, they are not analytically vulnerable. While they do not in the aggregate amount to a generalizable proposition, they do not conflict with each other. They are not inconsistent, they are separate. And they are articulated and undisguised. As such they stand in contrast to the erratic and apparently inarticulable subjectivity of the Court's obscenity decisions.

It is notorious that the famous clear-and-present-danger test, first enunciated by Holmes in cases arising during the First World War,* states rather than solves a free-speech problem. The point is best put in an oft-quoted passage of Professor Paul A. Freund: "The truth is that the clear-and-present danger test is an oversimplified judgment unless it takes account also of a number of other factors: the relative seriousness of the danger in comparison with the value of the occasion for speech or political activity; the availability of more moderate controls than those which the state has imposed; and perhaps the specific intent with which the speech or activity is launched. No matter how rapidly we utter the phrase 'clear and present danger,' or how closely we hyphenate the words, they are not a substitute for the weighing of values."[65]

* See *supra*, p. 27.

The basic proposition is that the First Amendment need not prevent government from regulating speech that impinges on other legitimate interests. But the value of speech and the other interests that government may be concerned to protect must be balanced, and this is the judicial task. As early as 1939, in *Schneider* v. *State*,[66] the Court held that the perfectly valid interest in keeping streets clean and unlittered would not support ordinances absolutely prohibiting the distribution of handbills—although the interest in the movement of traffic, for example, would justify an ordinance forbidding soap-box speeches in the middle of an intersection. "Mere legislative preferences or beliefs respecting matters of public convenience," the Court said, "may well support regulation directed at other personal activities, but be insufficient to justify such as diminishes the exercise of rights so vital to the maintenance of democratic institutions." In cases dealing with the right to associate or the right to demonstrate, rather than with what may be thought of as more purely speech, the Warren Court carried this process of balancing forward.[67]

The same kind of judgment is required, in circumstances that vary only slightly, if at all, when symbolic speech, as it has been called, is involved, as in cases of protest-cum-civil-disobedience that have been arising of late. The concept of symbolic speech means no more than that gestures or other acts, not only words, may be methods of communication, so that when someone performs an otherwise harmless act, such as hanging out a red flag or standing mute, he will be considered to have spoken, and be entitled to invoke the First Amendment.[68] When the action that is intended to communicate has consequences other than communication, it is speech nonetheless, if it is indeed meant to communicate, and it is at the same time conduct that may impinge on other interests of the society. Whether it may be forbidden depends on the weight that is assigned to the interest to be protected by forbidding it. The action is only conduct, and not speech, if its purpose is not to communicate, but to gain some other independent and exclusive objective.

Now when a man publicly burns or turns in his draft card, his purpose obviously is not to evade the draft. It is to communicate his protest. The act is senseless otherwise. Such cases, therefore, concern speech. The first question is whether this form of speech may be suppressed in the service of the government's interest to preserve the draft cards and to ensure that registrants have them in their possession. The further question is whether, even if the balance so far is struck in favor of speech, the act of turning-in or burning a draft card impinges on some other interest that government may legitimately wish to protect. But in respect even of the first, and certainly of the second question, burning and turning-in are distinguishable acts. Upholding a conviction for draft-card burning in *United States* v. *O'Brien*,[69] the Warren Court, in a remarkably bland opinion, seemed to answer both questions in favor of the government. One can understand the result, and perhaps it is right, but the case ought not be regarded as concluding the different case of a turn-in.

Plainly the Court decided that the interest of the government in seeing to it that each registrant carries a draft card on his person is not trivial, and it considered that this interest outweighs the value of speech which takes the form of a public burning of a draft card. An act such as this is different in temper from a peaceable turn-in. A public burning of even so small an object as a draft card may be viewed as a quasi-violent act. It may also, like flag burning, be seen as offensive; indecent behavior in public being a not inappropriate analogy.

At the argument of the *O'Brien* case, Chief Justice Warren asked: "What if a soldier in Vietnam, in a crowd, broke his weapon? Would it be symbolic speech?" And Justice Fortas asked whether the act of throwing a rock through a window of the White House could claim First Amendment protection, and whether "if a person lies down on a railroad track to block the passage of a train" the action could be considered symbolic speech? The interests touched on by these varying actions differ, and may in differing measures be entitled to protection by the government. "Am I correct in understanding that you are saying that draft-card burning is essentially a form of communication that does not hurt others and does not interfere with any legitimate governmental function?"— Mr. Justice Fortas, summarizing the previous questioning, finally asked counsel for O'Brien. Counsel's answer was yes, and in the *O'Brien* case the Court's answer was no.[70] But to hold that the burning of a draft card interferes with a legitimate government interest in the cards themselves, and with an interest in public order, and may, therefore, be forbidden, is not necessarily to hold—because the balance of values may be different—that a peaceable turn-in of draft cards, which has a similar, but even so not precisely the same, effect on the government's interest in the card itself, and which has a quite dissimilar effect on the government's interest in the maintenance of public order, may also be forbidden.

I have dwelt on the Warren Court's refusal, too often, to submit to the discipline of the analytically tenable distinction, and I have dwelt on other failings of a like character. The insistence on reason in the judicial process, on analytical coherence, and on principled judgment no matter how narrow its compass,* is traditional. Despite the countless lapses, it is an unmistakable thread in the fabric of our law—not alone the law of the Constitution— and of its literature. Despite their own lapses, as when Frankfurter exalted the result and discounted the opinion in the *Pipe Line Cases,* the Progressive realists from whom the Warren Court traced its lineage did not waver

---

* A principled decision, to use a formulation of Professor Herbert Wechsler, is one that rests "with respect to every step that is involved in reaching judgment on analysis and reasons quite transcending the immediate result that is achieved." Constitutional provisions, as Mr. Wechsler concedes, are "directed to protecting certain values"; they permit the judges, moreover, one may add, to stress or single out certain values, or even to generate them. And "the principled development of a particular [constitutional] provision is concerned with the value or values thus involved." Principled decision making means "that a value and its measure [are] determined by a general analysis that gives no weight to accidents of application, finding a scope that is acceptable whatever interest, group, or person may assert the claim. So, too, when there is conflict among values having constitutional protection, calling for their ordering or accommodation . . . the principle of resolution must be neutral in a comparable sense (both in the definition of the individual competing values and in the approach that it entails to value competition)." H. Wechsler, *Principles, Politics and Fundamental Law,* 5, xiii–xiv (1961).

in their allegiance to the method of reason, witness their proclamation of a "science of law." They used reason to put in question old values, and they came to the realization that their own were not to be found in reason alone. But they never put in question the value of rigorous analysis; indeed, they sought to restore it to its rightful place. They were in this sense also men of the Enlightenment, holding to reason as a civilizing force, and holding that clarity and candor, what Felix Frankfurter called the "conscious recognition of the nature" of the process, tend to be warrantors of validity, or at least of quality.

The restraints of reason tend to ensure also the independence of the judge, to liberate him from the demands and fears—dogmatic, arbitrary, irrational, self- or group-centered—that so often enchain other public officials. They make it possible for the judge, on some occasions, at any rate, to oppose against the will and faith of others, not merely his own will or deeply-felt faith, but a method of reaching judgments that may command the allegiance, on a second thought, even of those who find a result disagreeable. The judge is thus buttressed against the world, but what is perhaps more significant and certain, against himself, against his own natural tendency to give way before waves of feeling and opinion that may be as momentary as they are momentarily overwhelming.

The obverse of the assurance of independence in the judge is the justification that his pursuit of the method of reason may provide for his supreme autonomy. Constitutional judgment is a high policy-making function performed in a political democracy by an institution that has to be regarded as deviant. For purposes of its one-man, one-vote doctrine, the Supreme Court has, paradoxically enough, persuaded itself that our government is organized on the populist principle. This is an admission against interest on the part of the Court. Nevertheless, our government is not, and ought not be, strictly majoritarian.

The Madisonian model of a multiplicity of factions vying against each other and checking each other still more nearly fits our system, which retains traces of resemblance even to Calhoun's model of concurrent majorities. It is perfectly clear as well that, aside from the judges, many other elites that are not immediately and not directly controlled by the electoral process wield power in American government. Yet elections do influence, and sometimes they determine, the movement of public policy, the policy of the nonjudicial elites as well as that of the immediately responsive officials. And the prospect of elections that may be so determinative has vast influence in the intervals between, for the electorate puts men in office and deposes them, including ultimately members of elites.

But elections are the tip of the iceberg; the bulk of the political process is below. The jockeying, the bargaining, the trading, the threatening and the promising, the checking and the balancing, the spurring and the vetoing are continuous. They not only form the environment of government, legislative and executive, elected and elite, they are its engine. The judges are insulated from this environment, and secure against its influence, as well as against the influence of elections. The judges' engine in some aspects of their function is legislative policy, which they must find and execute; in others it is themselves.

83

The independence of the judges is an absolute requirement if individual justice is to be done, if a society is to
ensure that individuals will be dealt with in accordance
with duly enacted general policies of the society, not by
the whim of officials or of mobs, and dealt with even-
handedly, under rules that would apply also to others
similarly situated, no matter who they might be. The
methods of reason and the norms of the craft of law
bolster this independence. We rightly protest when it is
lacking, as it was in the *Rosenberg* case,* and as, for
different reasons, it was in Ralph Ginzburg's. But supreme
judicial autonomy, the judge answerable only to his own
conscience in making policy for the society, in adjusting,
conformably to one or another choice of values, the conflicting interests, desires, and ethical and moral aspira-
tions and preferences of the groups that constitute the
society—that is something else again, even though men,
using the words in a different sense, may call various
choices of policy just or unjust. The words are used in a
different sense now because they are no longer rooted in a
single, well-recognized ethical precept; and because
groups, as opposed to individuals, have access to political
power in a system that governs, as Professor Robert Dahl
has said, by minorities rule.[71]

Access to political power is not a function solely of the
franchise, just as the franchise, even for groups that have
and exercise it to the full, does not provide all the access
and leverage that intensity of interest, conviction, or

* See *supra*, p. 5.

grievance may demand and justify. But the franchise is important, and symbolically it is crucial. Hence the premise of a system of "minorities rule" is invalid, and an assessment of the judicial function based on that premise is faulty, to the extent that the vote is denied to any group in predestined terms—in terms which foreclose individual mobility, and which are grounded, not in a rational judgment about qualifications for voting, such as literacy, but in a prejudice attaching to the individual at birth. The business of the Court is not to become the instrument for attaining the substantive objectives of such an excluded group, but to nullify the exclusion, as in the case of the Negroes the Court has in recent times consistently striven to do, pursuant to the mandate of the Fifteenth Amendment.[72] (The Nineteenth Amendment, guaranteeing the vote to women, has happily proved self-executing.)

Access is fatally impeded as well, in a manner also vitiating the premise of a system of "minorities rule," if any group is subjected to disabilities that amount to banishment from the body politic, if a group is, in effect, proscribed, outlawed, whether or not it formally retains the franchise. Such a group may be defined in terms of race or ethnic origin, or otherwise denominated—it is all the same, so long as the proscription does not fall on the individual because of some unlawful act he has committed or participated in committing, but entirely on account of his membership in the group.

When Japanese Americans were effectively proscribed during World War II, evacuated from the West Coast, and detained, the Court did not bestir itself.[73] The Court has been somewhat more sensitive since, in somewhat comparable circumstances, suggesting that mere membership in the Communist Party cannot be made a crime.[74] And at the end of the Vinson years, the Court perceived that private forces within the society, having no control of public force, may nevertheless exert themselves quite efficiently to proscribe one or another group, and that the First Amendment ought not to stand in the way of efforts by the state to punish and prevent, as by group libel laws, the spreading of incendiary falsehoods about racial or religious groups, and the promotion of strife which tends "to obstruct the manifold adjustments required for free, ordered life in a metropolitan, polyglot community."[75]

Putting aside, then, justice to the individual, and the function, so seldom in issue, of guarding the elemental integrity of a system in which all groups have access to political power, the supreme autonomy that the Court asserts in many matters of substantive policy needs justification in a political democracy. And it can have it, if at all, only in the claim that the function never relinquishes the pursuit of reason, and that ultimately it is principled, that the Court does not discharge its office even by doing what most people may think is right or necessary, unless it does it in principled fashion. The justification must be that constitutional judgment turns on issues of moral philosophy and political theory, which we abstract from the common political process, at least initially, because it would be wrong to decide them merely by a count of noses, or by striking some bargain.

To be sure, no formal method of reasoning from axioms will answer questions of moral philosophy and political theory plainly and definitively, but it will help answer them differently than a process open to trials of strength, and to the free play of interest, predilection, and prejudice. And it will help test answers against analogues in the tradition of the society and in surrounding contemporary practice. Leaving some value choices to judges who rest decision on principle may meet a need for continuity and harmony in our values. Judicial supremacy is necessarily intended as a conservative device even when it serves as an instrument of change—particularly then, perhaps.

Certainly the Court, like other institutions, is in part the maker of the tradition that influences it, and other institutions are also constrained in some measure by the history they have made. And certainly history is more a storehouse of caveats than of patented remedies for the ills of mankind. But while the other institutions may be, the Court is not the place for the heedless break with the past, not the place for the half loaf that is better than none, for the split difference and other arbitrary choices, or for the action supported by nothing but rhetoric, sentiment, anger, or prejudice. The Court is the place for principled judgment, disciplined by the method of reason familiar to the discourse of moral philosophy, and in constitutional adjudication, the place only for that, or else its insulation from the political process is inexplicable.

If a constitutional function insulated from politics is so explained, however, it is still all too feebly justified. Like other statesmen, judges must generate norms. Special conditions are created to enhance the quality of their performance. They are thus rendered unresponsive, and in a society which subjects other statesmen, who generate some not dissimilar norms, to political checks and controls, the absence of all such checks and controls in the case of the judges continues to pose a question. It continues to pose a question particularly since history shows that the judges' norms, like those of other statesmen, are by no means all of permanent validity.

The answer is that, in their own way, the judges are subject to controls similar to those that operate on other policy-making elites, and that additional political checks are built into the judicial function as well. In a celebrated essay a little more than a decade ago, Mr. Dahl discovered what most lawyers thought they knew anyway—as is so often the case with political scientists—but he said it and supported it systematically, which is no trivial achievement, and is too infrequently the case with lawyers. He discovered that over time the Supreme Court speaks for and with the dominant political alliance. The appointment power, which is political, ensures as much.[76]

But the appointment power is a blunt instrument. If it operates politically, it does so fallibly, by projecting its guesses into the future. And it is sometimes constrained and inhibited. Remnants of the old style of Constitution and judge worship, which denied the propriety of appointments based on secular, political considerations, or at least the propriety of frank public ventilation of the political nature of an appointment—remnants of this style sometimes afflict politicians, and may be observed in other, more surprising quarters as well; and they induce a certain caution in the appointment process.

We can't look "for men with certain creeds on property," Taft said to Brandeis, who thought Taft knew better.* And in truth Taft did know better, but in 1909–12, when he made six appointments, Taft was not only ambivalent about his political motivation, but inhibited in giving it free rein. And when an effective, if not dominant, political alliance in the Senate, feeling that Justice Fortas was out of tune with it, resisted his nomination as Chief Justice in 1968, certain leaders of the Bar attacked not only the validity of the Senators' claim to represent an alliance dominant in the country at large, but also the legitimacy of standards for confirmation going beyond the nominee's professional competence, and taking account of his views on matters of policy.

Justice Fortas himself was clear that his opinions were open to Senatorial inquiry, and that agreement or disagreement with them was relevant—although in order to protect his independence as a sitting judge he wisely refused to enlarge orally on his decisions, or refused for the most part to do so. But, like past confirmation struggles, the episode of Justice Fortas' nomination brought forth no perfect, and no universal, assent to what would seem the obviously correct proposition, necessary to Mr. Dahl's point, which Senator Strom Thurmond of South Carolina stated (wisdom can issue even from so egregious a source): "In view of the Court's enormous influence and relative lack of checks on the Court, I believe the deci-

* See *supra*, p. 17.

sions of the Court . . . are determining in deciding whether or not to confirm a Justice or Chief Justice."[*][77]

In any event, even if, despite qualifications and aberrations, the appointment process does over time tend to bring the Court and reigning political alliances into harmony, and if over time the general political climate and the judges' good common sense have the same effect, there is often a period of dissonance until a newly-forged political alliance catches up with the Court, or vice versa, and the consequences can be as serious as they nearly were in the Court-packing fight of 1937.

Over time, moreover, in the very long run, as Keynes remarked, we shall all be dead. What is more important, therefore, than Mr. Dahl's findings is that in the immediate aspect also the society is not without recourse. The Supreme Court's judgments may be put forth as universally prescriptive; but they actually become so only when they gain widespread assent. They bind of their own force no one but the parties to a litigation. To realize the promise that all others similarly situated will be similarly bound, the Court's judgments need the assent and the cooperation first of the political institutions, and ultimately of the people.

This is an untidy proposition, for its truth varies some-

[*] Senate and President are, however, partners in the appointment process. Both are properly concerned with policy and ideology, but the Constitution gives the initiative to the President. When Senate and President differ to the point where the ideological clash between a nominee and a Senate majority is violent, the Senate is well within its rights to reject a nomination, and it has done so on occasion. Yet the Senate must not demand precisely the ideological profile it would prefer, for then the appointment process will be in deadlock.

what as the specific immediate addressees of any given Supreme Court decision vary. If the addressees are relatively few, as in voting decrees issued under the Fifteenth Amendment, and in reapportionment decisions, the judiciary is in a relatively better position all by itself to render its law operational, although it took an Act of Congress,[78] we should not forget, finally to enfranchise large numbers of Southern Negroes. When the addressees are many, as in the school segregation and school prayer cases, the judiciary by itself tends to be relatively helpless.

But there is another difference between the voting and especially the reapportionment cases, on the one hand, and the school segregation and prayer cases, on the other. The first set of decisions met with a great deal more and readier acceptance on the part of the general public than the second, and therein lies the ultimate secret of effective judicial law, and very probably, in our system, of any effective law at all, whatever its source.

Virtually all important decisions of the Supreme Court are the beginnings of conversations between the Court and the people and their representatives. They are never, at the start, conversations between equals. The Court has an edge, because it initiates things with some immediate action, even if limited. But conversations they are, and to say that the Supreme Court lays down the law of the land is to state the ultimate result, following upon a complex series of events, in some cases, and in others it is a form of speech only. The effectiveness of the judgment universalized depends on consent and administration.

The Court is often incapable of generating the necessary consent by itself, and it does not command the resources of administration. Thus for some six years following decision of *Brown* v. *Board of Education,* until at least 1960, the cooperation of the federal political institutions and the acquiescence of many state governments were seriously in doubt, to say the least, and it was hardly true that the case was the law of the land. Much has taken place since to change that situation, but even now the effectiveness of *Brown* as law largely depends on the will and the resources that are brought to its administration, and these are in the control, not of the Court, but of the political institutions in the states and in Washington.

Compare with *Brown* the Court's decisions forbidding religious prayers in public schools as violations of the Establishment Clause. There has been very little in the way of general assent to .these decisions, not only in a single recalcitrant region, but throughout the country,[79] and no dedicated, nationwide institutional litigant has taken them up, as the NAACP, of course, took up *Brown.* The cooperation of state and federal political bodies has been virtually nil. It is difficult to imagine a Presidential candidate promising to banish prayer from the public schools, as John F. Kennedy in 1960—and Richard Nixon, too—promised to banish segregation. And so the effectiveness of the prayer decisions as operational law in our society is very minor indeed, and would be, even if an institutional litigant were pressing for their enforcement.

Again, the Court's procedural decisions in criminal cases, many of which are intended to govern police behavior, have long been less than fully effective in practice. There has been little the Court could do about it. For a season, it seemed as if the executive department of the federal government was aligning itself with the Court in the effort to persuade our people that crime is a social phenomenon with causes of its own, and that the level of crime does not rise or fall in direct relation to the rate at which the criminal process puts people in jail—or, as George Wallace used to say, under a jail. True crime control measures were proposed and passed—grant-in-aid programs aimed at professionalizing police work—which may in the long run help convince our people that the criminal process can be most efficacious by being decent and principled rather than rough and ready.

This situation no longer prevails, however. In the Crime Control and Safe Streets Act of 1968[80]—which contains the grant-in-aid programs just mentioned—Congress also repudiated some of the Court's most recent criminal cases, specifically *Miranda* v. *Arizona,*[81] dealing with station-house confessions, and *United States* v. *Wade,*[82] dealing with line-ups for eye-witness identification. And the Senate's non-action in 1968 on the nomination of Justice Fortas to be Chief Justice, while subject to several interpretations and qualifications, was at least in part an expression of dissatisfaction with the Court's decisions in criminal cases. What is most important, just as the election of 1960 was a vote of ratification of the Court's holding in *Brown* v. *Board of Education* as then understood, so the election of 1968 may have been something of a vote of repudiation of the criminal decisions—partial perhaps, fraught with misunderstanding, altogether regrettable and hopefully reversible—but something of a vote of repudiation. The Court is, and ought to be, more apt to dig in its heels on issues of criminal procedure than on matters of more substantive policy, but it is surely likely that the Court's law will be increasingly ineffective, unless the political verdict against it is reversed.

Friend and foe of the Court alike, the one in wish-fulfillment, the other out of fear or in order to provoke fear, constantly inflate the Court's supposed power. The lawyers among observers of the Court seem to approach its decisions in obedience to the ancient rule of equity: they regard that as done which ought to be done, because the Court has said so. And historians surveying the past, and political scientists presumably probing the present, often fall into the same error. But the untutored know better, or often act, or fail to act, as if they knew better, and they are more numerous.

The Court's effectiveness, it is often remarked, depends substantially on confidence, on what is called prestige. It is likely, therefore—the proposition has never previously had a real empirical test, but the Warren Court may have provided one—that there is a natural quantitative limit to the number of major, principled interventions the Court can permit itself per decade, let us say. It is a matter of credibility. Will anyone who is not in a revolutionary state of wholesale disillusionment with the society continue to believe that basic principle is in question if the Court puts it in question every other Monday? And will anyone whose frame of mind is one of total disillusionment with the system be long content to take his principles from the Court? Revolutionaries are not a reliable constituency for judges.

Again, there must eventually be a limit to the number of judicially-pronounced principles that the political institutions will have the will to make their own and the energy to execute, as they have in large measure accepted and executed the reapportionment and segregation decisions. A Court unmindful of this limit will find that more and more of its pronouncements are unfulfilled promises, which will ultimately discredit and denude the function of constitutional adjudication.

This is what Justice Frankfurter had in mind when he worried out loud at one of the arguments of *Brown* v. *Board of Education* that nothing could be worse than an abstract judicial declaration which remains abstract and is evaded.* There is much that could be worse than one such declaration, but nothing indeed could be worse than many. It follows also, quite aside from quantitative limits, that before committing itself to a principle which may have to remain abstract, or worse yet, be repudiated, the Court is well advised to test public opinion, since it can better suffer the kind of withdrawal that consists of not going forward than the kind that consists of visibly retreating.

Such considerations, flowing from the Court's position in the political scheme of things, are in tension with the methods of reason and principle that alone justify the exercise of supreme judicial power in a political democracy. For these considerations invite the Court not only to define principle in the narrowest possible compass (to abhor absolutes, as Holmes and Frankfurter counseled), but also to take cautious steps from limit to limit, to approach principles of judgment through a line-drawing

* See *supra*, p. 6.

process, case by case. It is because of its sense of these considerations that the Court again and again confronts the choice between a coherent principle, and its arbitrary limitation.

Whatever failings of the Warren Court may be attributed to simple inadequacy of performance, which is partly explained, in turn, by the press of too great a volume of important business, here, in these aspects of the Court's political position, as my colleague Jan G. Deutsch has well argued,[83] is the systemic cause of breakdowns in the process of principled judgment; not a necessary cause —the breakdowns are not unavoidable—but the systemic one.

The process of the coherent, analytically warranted, principled declaration of general norms alone justifies the Court's function, and yet it is at the same time a source of danger to the survival of the institution in a society which, if driven to demand ultimate consistency, will find it in the practices of political democracy, not in submission to the Court's authority. The Court provoked relatively mild political opposition when it was making relatively narrow decisions in confession, right-to-counsel, and like criminal-procedure cases. It headed into trouble after the strongly, and as one may think soundly, principled decision in *Miranda* v. *Arizona*. The obscenity cases have also aroused opposition in Congress. They had a significant role in the struggle in 1968 over the nomination of Justice Fortas to be Chief Justice. But it was secondary to the role of the criminal-procedure decisions. Does any surmise make sense other than that the opposition to the obscenity cases would have been more widespread had the Court announced a strong principle rather than floundering about, as it has done, and even coming down on the side of suppression in the *Mishkin* and *Ginzburg*[84] decisions?

The Court's harshest rationalist critics do not, with respect to many of the cases they object to, regret the Court's failure to adopt the most principled and far-reaching rationales of decision,[85] nor do they necessarily quarrel with the results in terms of their own sympathies and policy preferences. They do counsel the Court to forgo action if no principled basis for it can be found, and thus to halt movement in one or another direction of progress. But this is expensive advice, and it is natural to question, therefore, the insistence on principle, perhaps even always on reason, on analytical rigor, purity, some would say mere elegance, especially since on occasion, on the occasion, no doubt, also of this book, reasonable men may differ about the conclusions to be drawn from the most rigorous attempt at analysis itself. Even when the law pretends to be a science, it is not, after all, mathematics.

Answering, or rather refusing to answer, in *Jones* v. *Mayer Co.*, which concerned racial segregation in housing,* an analytical point made in dissent by Justices Harlan and White, Mr. Justice Douglas protested against "allowing the legal mind to draw lines and make distinctions that have no place in the jurisprudence of a nation striving to rejoin the human race."[86] Few would quite adopt this emotional, not to say anti-intellectual tone, but many nevertheless might question whether the price of

* See *supra*, p. 49.

craftsmanship is not too high when it is exacted in the discriminatory refusal to sell a house to a Negro, in continuation of the poll tax, in denying the vote to Spanish-speaking Puerto Ricans in New York, or in the possible execution of a Witherspoon.

If in such cases analysis has not been used with the requisite skill to locate the point at which a value judgment is called for, if that judgment has been fudged or disguised, if history has been used unjustifiably as a crutch, it is nevertheless clear what the Court has identified as the general direction of progress, where its sympathies and preferences lie, and is that not good enough? We know what the result means even if its full significance is not as plain as it might be, and as to that, the next case will tell; indeed it will tell, these days, soon enough.

The values of reason and the demands of and for principle are what they are. For myself, I continue to believe with my teacher, the late Professor Henry M. Hart, Jr., that if judicial supremacy is at all justifiable, then it is because the Court is "predestined in the long run not only by the thrilling tradition of Anglo-American law but also by the hard facts of its position in the structure of American institutions to be a voice of reason, charged with the creative function of discerning afresh and of articulating and developing impersonal and durable principles."[87]

I have argued elsewhere in detail[88] that the cost of such a commitment, as reflected in the result of this or that case, need not be prohibitive. The tension between principle and the hard—at any rate, often ominous—facts of the day's politics can be resolved. There are ways consistent with reason to avoid results that run counter to the direction in which the Court believes it should move, even though, on occasion, to be sure, the judges must abide the disagreeable result, and there is thus a price to be paid in terms of action they must forgo. I think it is worth paying. I have come to doubt in many instances the Court's capacity to develop "durable principles," and to doubt, therefore, that judicial supremacy can work and is tolerable in broad areas of social policy. Yet, if and where judicial supremacy can work, the Hartian prescription, I believe, is of the essence. Given the Court's position both in "the structure of American institutions," and in the political scheme of things from time to time, my guess is that in the end the highest price will be exacted for sounds of unreason made by "the voice of reason."

But the Justices of the Warren Court placed their own bet on the future, even as their more analytical and scientific progenitors, who were Mr. Hart's teachers, also did. If the bet pays off, whatever their analytical failings, the Justices will have won everything—for the moment, at any rate. *Brown* v. *Board of Education,* Mr. Wechsler has said, has "the best chance of making an enduring contribution to the quality of our society of any [decision] that I know in recent years."[89] Should that chance materialize, it isn't going to matter that Mr. Wechsler thought that the decision rested on an inadequately neutral principle, or that its reasoning is otherwise faulty, or fails to take account of all that is relevant.

In such cases as those dealing with the poll tax and with the vote for Spanish-speaking Puerto Ricans, the ultimate issue is whether we value variety, and hence wish to permit states to set qualifications for voting within broad limits, whether we value federated experimentation and the sense of local independence, or whether we care more about expanding a uniform national electorate. There is opinion both ways, and the tendency of opinion in the Warren Court was obvious. If it prevails, little else will matter. The same is true of the almost unbroken tendency of the Warren Court's decisions in legislative apportionment, racial and criminal cases, the principled decisions and the ill-reasoned ones, those that do and those that do not make specious use of historical materials. It would be intellectual megalomania not to concede that the Warren Court, like Marshall's, may for a time have been an institution seized of a great vision, that it may have glimpsed the future, and gained it.

Conceding as much—that "history has little tolerance for any of those reasonable judgments that have turned out to be wrong"—Mr. Wechsler added that the verdicts of history are unfathomable in advance, and that history "is never a contemporary critic."[90] That statement was made a decade ago. Owing perhaps to the rate at which the Court has wreaked itself upon the society since then, and to the rate at which the society as a whole seems to be hurtling toward its future, history may now more nearly serve as a contemporary critic. And perhaps another scenario of the future than that implicit in the work of the Warren Court is worth examining.

Chapter 4

Remembering the Future

As I have suggested,* following Professor Kurland, a broadly-conceived egalitarianism was the main theme in the music to which the Warren Court marched. It was evident, of course, in the racial cases, in decisions leveling qualifications for voting, and in those decreeing equal apportionment on a one-man, one-vote basis. And the egalitarian melody was strong in procedural decisions, chiefly criminal, seeking to minimize the disadvantages to which the poor are subject.[1] Two accompanying themes were the enlargement of the dominion of law and the centralization in national institutions of the law-giving function.

The Warren Court was quick to impose the same norms

* See *supra*, p. 13.

on state and national governments alike. In dealing with the obscenity problem, for example, the Court would not heed Mr. Justice Harlan's plea that separate rules might be made applicable to the federal government and to state and local governments.[2] Yet the dangers of national censorship are not the same as the dangers of local suppression. The federal government is apt to impose the standards of Dubuque on Greenwich Village, whereas Dubuque can impose them only in Dubuque. Again, in its decisions on criminal procedure—decisions concerning, for example, unreasonable searches and seizures—the Warren Court sought to enforce national uniformity in every detail, without regard, so to speak, to varieties of criminal experience.[3]

In pursuit of the ideal of equality, the Warren Court all too often assimilated private behavior to government action; it not only forbade, of course, as had its predecessors, discrimination at the hands of the state, or of any unit of government, but was keen to detect the hand of the state in private discriminations.[*] In the Warren era, moreover, as to a degree also in the heyday of the old faith at the turn of the century and after, a general tendency was noticeable to circumscribe and displace private ordering, to legalize the society, to rationalize it in the sense in which the great industrial consolidators spoke of rationalizing the economy, to impose order on the market of norms, values, and institutions. There was evidence, particularly in the subordinate federal courts, of an imperfectly bridled managerial drive.

[*] See *e.g., supra*, pp. 65–69.

A certain habit of command, an impatience to take charge of unruly affairs and impose a solution that seems apt, comes as readily to judges as to other able men of good intentions who are in a position to work their will. It came readily enough to the judges of the early decades of this century, who intervened routinely in labor disputes, for example, and in controversies concerning rates and services between public utilities and various states and municipalities. Rebuking—as it rarely did—a somewhat overzealous judge in such a case in 1910, the Supreme Court quoted the remark of an English Vice-Chancellor: "I am not sitting here as a Committee of Public Safety, armed with arbitrary power to prevent what it is said will be a great injury not to Birmingham only but to the whole of England; that is not my function."[4] But it is a function that judges are prone to assume, and to which they were increasingly encouraged by the reach the Warren Court gave to law, and by the expectations that were thus induced.

The long arm of modern law may be observed fully extended in *Application of President and Directors of Georgetown College, Inc.,*[5] and in *United States* v. *George.*[6] These cases are examples of what I have in mind, even though they are set apart, perhaps, by the peculiarly painful nature of their circumstances; but they are suggestive and symptomatic. In both cases Jehovah's Witnesses voluntarily entered hospitals for treatment of bleeding ulcers, and in due course, at a time when in the judgment of attending physicians failure to administer blood transfusions would have been fatal, refused their consent to such transfusions for reasons of conscience dictated by their religion. In both cases the patient signed a form releasing the hospital from all liability for the consequences of failure to administer a transfusion, and in neither case was the position of the patient and his family that they would under all circumstances oppose and resist a transfusion. The position was merely that they could not give their consent to one. It was the act of consenting that violated conscience, not necessarily the administration of foreign blood without their consent. In both cases federal judges hastily summoned to the scene signed orders authorizing the transfusions.

Failure of the courts "to declare the law," said Judge J. Skelly Wright in the *Georgetown* case, "would not place the responsibility for decision in the executive or legislative branches of the government. Judicial abdication would create a legal vacuum to be filled only by the notions, and remedies, of the private parties themselves." That of course is precisely the point. As Judge Warren E. Burger, the present Chief Justice of the United States, then a judge of the Court of Appeals for the District of Columbia, said in dissent, doctors and hospitals are often confronted with nice professional and ethical problems, as are numerous other groups and institutions in the society. The "notions, and remedies, of the private parties" constitute what is compendiously known as the system of private ordering.

The institutions of the private sector—economic or professional—can be too large, unresponsive, and oppressive. The remedy then is not necessarily to create a superstructure of public institutions charged with governing the private ones, for the superstructure is apt to be even larger, and equally oppressive. Legislation can attempt, rather, to control the size of private institutions, and it can prescribe modes and procedures, and perhaps substantive standards, for their exercise of power over individuals. Private ordering can also break down in group conflict, and judges as well as legislators, in whose charge is the public order, may be constrained to declare resolving and governing law. Legislators, it may be, ultimately always. But not necessarily judges.[7] And to do so after an attempt at private ordering has been made, to do so, this is to say, in a suit for damages after the fact, is to be in a position to ratify or modify the private ordering that has taken place, and to judge the experience. It is very different from making the initial decision, thus arrogating the entire responsibility, from beginning to end, and freeing the private institutions of any portion of it.

One may wonder how effective, how good and how acceptable to the society, such decision-making by judges —generalists, necessarily less well-informed than they might be by their episodic interventions—will prove, and this is a question I mean to raise. But my emphasis now is on the enveloping conception of law as the sole system of ordering that such decisions bespeak. The Warren Court's tendency to disenthrall itself from jurisdictional fetters is a function of this conception of law. The Court has not by any means taken on all that has been pressed on it. It has declined opportunities to pass on the constitutionality of the President's actions in Vietnam.[8] It has not dispensed with the need for a lawsuit; it is still, unlike the President or the Congress, a passive body that must wait for a litigant to move it to action. But in such decisions as *Flast*

v. *Cohen* and *South Carolina* v. *Katzenbach*,° the Court has substantially loosened the definition of a lawsuit, it has opened the door wider to more litigants, and has indeed come near to making the lawsuit something of a formality, still an expensive one, but within the reach of just about all who can afford it, at just about any time of their choice.

In assuming the power, like a legislature, to set an arbitrary date for the coming into effect of its decisions, the Warren Court further enlarged its freedom to address an ever-widening range of the society's problems, and to pronounce applicable law. The Court assumed this power, as we have seen, with respect to a number of its decisions concerning criminal procedure, which it did not allow to be, as is unusual, wholly retroactive, but which it did not announce for solely prospective application either. To have announced them altogether prospectively would have run the risk of stemming the flow of litigation, the Court said, since "the incentive of counsel to advance contentions requiring a change in the law" might have been decreased.[9] Without running this risk, then—a telling and characteristic precaution—the Court liberated itself from the restraint naturally imposed by the retroactivity of decisions, which can work out inequitably, or otherwise in alarming fashion, and hence gives pause.

Another of the principal themes of the Warren Court, related to the egalitarian, legalitarian, and centralizing themes, was majoritarianism. The Court found the essence of political democracy in the power of a majority to

° See *supra*, pp. 63–65, 58–59.

impose its wishes through an election, except, to be sure, as the sway of the majority is limited by law. This is the meaning of the one-man, one-vote rule of the apportionment cases. It is the meaning also, in part, of the decisions enlarging the electorate and leveling qualifications for voting, as is shown by Justice Douglas' citation of the apportionment cases in *Harper* v. *Virginia Board of Elections*, the poll-tax decision. *

The main statement of the Court's position came in *Reynolds* v. *Sims.* Chief Justice Warren's opinion for the Court spoke of individual equality. One man's vote ought not to be worth more than another's. But there was great emphasis also, in *Reynolds* v. *Sims* and in the rest of the apportionment cases, on a statistical showing that malapportionment enabled a minority of voters to control a legislature, or under the Georgia county-unit system, elect a governor. The Chief Justice proclaimed: "Legislators represent people, not trees or acres. Legislators are elected by voters, not farms or cities or economic interests. . . . Logically, in a society ostensibly grounded on representative government, it would seem reasonable that a majority of the people of a State could elect a majority of that State's legislators. To conclude differently, and to sanction minority control of state legislative bodies, would appear to deny majority rights in a way that far surpasses any possible denial of minority rights that might otherwise be thought to result. Since legislatures are responsible for enacting laws by which all citizens are to be governed, they should be bodies which are collectively

* See *supra,* pp. 59–60.

responsive to the popular will." And the Chief Justice laid it down explicitly that "economic or other sorts of group interests" were not factors that could constitutionally be taken into account in apportioning a legislature. "Citizens, not history or economic interests, cast votes," he said.[10] In Colorado, a substantial majority of the voters had by referendum approved a departure from the one-man, one-vote standard. Even the majority itself, the Court held, cannot deprive itself of the right to rule as a majority.[11]

Populist majoritarianism, not some complex checked and balanced Madisonian adjustment among countervailing groups and factions, leading to the rule by minorities that Robert Dahl describes—populist majoritarianism was the principle of the apportionment cases. "Missouri contends," said the Court, disposing of a Congressional districting controversy in 1969, "that [population] variances were necessary to avoid fragmenting areas with distinct economic and social interests and thereby diluting the effective representation of those interests in Congress. But to accept population variances, large or small, in order to create districts with specific interest orientations is antithetical to the basic premise of the constitutional command to provide equal representation for equal numbers of people."[12]

In *Fortson* v. *Morris*, the Court, dividing 5–4, allowed the Georgia legislature to elect as governor a candidate who had received a smaller portion of the popular vote than his opponent. An opinion by Justice Black drove to the result by main force, and made light of the apportionment decisions. Justice Black did not read them as necessarily resting on the majoritarian principle. They concerned merely, he said, the "equal right of 'all who participate in the election' to vote and have their votes counted without impairment or dilution."

Fortson v. *Morris* may be an *ad hoc* aberration, or it may foreshadow the eventual reduction of the apportionment decisions to triviality. In either event, it misstates their import. Justice Fortas, dissenting in *Fortson* v. *Morris*, was surely right in saying that the apportionment decisions could not have been intended as "merely much ado about form." The vote, said Justice Fortas, is "the basic instrument of democracy," and the apportionment decisions protected "not merely the casting of the vote or its mechanical counting . . . [but] the function—the office—the effect given to the vote." The vote, he continued, "is not an object of art. It is the sacred and most important instrument of democracy and of freedom. In simple terms, the vote is meaningless—it no longer serves the purpose of the democratic society—unless it, taken in the aggregate with the votes of other citizens, results in effecting the will of those citizens provided that they are more numerous than those of differing views. That is the meaning and effect of the great constitutional decisions of this Court."[13]

Majoritarianism is heady stuff. It is, in truth, a tide flowing with the swiftness of a slogan—whether popular sovereignty, as in the past, or one man, one vote, as in the Warren Court's formulation. The tide is apt to sweep over all institutions, seeking its level everywhere. Now that the Warren Court has released it again, it bids fair, for example, to engulf the Electoral College, even though on a less simplistic view of political arrangements, on a less obtrusively chaste view, that peculiar institution may be seen as performing a valuable function. The tide could well engulf the Court itself also.

Analytically, supreme judicial autonomy is not easily reconciled with any theory of political democracy, Madisonian or majoritarian. Judicial autonomy is sustained, not by a self-consistent theory, but by an ambivalent practical accommodation, and by a rhetorical tradition. The tradition, however, is Madisonian in tenor. It will be difficult to evolve a rhetoric of survival in a climate of uncompromising majoritarianism—as difficult for the judges as for the Electoral College. The Court fared rather ill with the Populists and other majoritarian political reformers of the Progressive Era. In times when Madisonian theory is in favor, it is at least rhetorically possible to defend the power of the judges by pointing to all manner of checks and balances, to the limited nature of all power, which signifies the intended inability of any group, including a majority, always to get everything it wants, and the intended ability of many groups, all of them minorities, to exercise vetoes; and by declaiming that our government is, after all, republican, not in the majoritarian sense democratic. It is not so easy to say all this when populist slogans are the order of the day, as the Warren Court's one-man, one-vote decisions have caused them to be. Thoroughgoing majoritarians, the Court may discover, are no more reliable a constituency for judges than revolutionaries, and the Court-induced reapportionment revolution may turn into an ironic triumph.

The Warren Court achieved a certain symmetry in its deployment of the majoritarian principle and of a concept of centralized and pervasive law; and it mistook this symmetry for theoretical consistency. (The symmetrical arrangement I speak of has at least the virtue of by-passing—even though, unfortunately, quite without dis-owning—the sophistry of arguments that the supremacy of the judges is consistent with democratic theory so long as the judges enhance the democratic process rather than restricting it, which is supposedly what they do in First Amendment and apportionment cases.) *

The Warren Court's implicit model of a government at once majoritarian and judicial had it that when indi-viduals and groups are unsuccessful in attaching them-selves to the ruling majority in a given constituency, or in getting satisfaction from it, they may appeal to the larger majority in the national constituency. This recourse the Court encouraged by enlarging the power of Congress under the Fourteenth Amendment, as for example in *Katzenbach* v. *Morgan.*† If no remedy is forthcoming even from the central majoritarian legislature, then the losers in the political process may appeal to the Court, which was consequently concerned to make itself more readily available than it had been in the past. As early as the argument of *Brown* v. *Board of Education,* the late Justice Robert H. Jackson, stating a fact rather than his own preference, remarked that the plaintiffs were in court because Congress would not act.‡

* See *supra,* pp. 34–38.

† See *supra,* pp. 48–49, 61–63.

‡ See *supra,* pp. 6–7.

Unmistakably the Warren Court considered itself under a special duty to act when recourse to Congress had failed or was likely to fail; and not unnaturally, for in a polity arranged on the majoritarian principle, and hence inescapably on the assumption that an identifiable majority exists at all times on most issues, and is coherent and relatively stable, the political process cannot be assumed to be accessible to all groups. In the Madisonian model, and one might say in purposefully malapportioned legislatures, most identifiable groups and interests in the society have access, and are likely to be able to maneuver for enough bargaining power to achieve at least some portion of their objectives. No such presumption is sensible in a more strictly majoritarian system.

It can be said, therefore, that the Warren Court's imposition of majoritarianism as the operative principle of political organization, and its conception of its own function were congruent. They met in the premise that the majoritarian process must, and perhaps if it works correctly will, produce certain results, which are given *a priori*. When it does not at the level of one constituency, it should be tried again at the higher level of another one. And when it doesn't at all, the Court will supply the deficiency. Madisonian theory also posits the possible miscarriage of the majoritarian process in a not dissimilar sense, and also has recourse to enlargement of the constituency. But it guards against miscarriages by diffusing and limiting power through the introduction of a series of non-majoritarian devices, and enlarges the constituency to this end. What the Warren Court crucially omitted to explain was why its model, unlike the Madisonian one, allowed for only a single locus of power countervailing that of the majority—the Court itself—and by reliance on the majoritarian principle forbade all others the Court could reach.

I am attempting now to identify and orchestrate the Warren Court's major themes; I am not now dealing with fragments of the music in one or another case, and not—to pursue a figure of Professor Kurland—with techniques of piano playing.* My object is not to formulate and defend the grounds of my own approval or disapproval—intellectual, moral, esthetic—although I should say that in my view the Court's majoritarianism is ill-conceived, egalitarianism is a worthy ideal but not in all circumstances a self-evident virtue, and centralized, unmitigatedly legalitarian government bears the seed of tyranny. But this is an assertion of ultimates put forward for revelatory rather than forensic purposes. And it is a parenthesis. My endeavor is to see whether the Warren Court's themes, whatever their worth as ultimates, were in harmony with each other, and whether they harmonized with so much of the future as contemporary history allows us to glimpse.

There are heard in the society dissonant themes; not voices of opposition or resistance to the Court's law, albeit

---

* "It behooves any critic of the Court's performance to close on a note reminiscent of the wall plaque of frontier times: 'Don't shoot the piano player. He's doing his best.' It is still possible, however, to wish that he would stick to the piano and not try to be a one-man band. It is too much to ask that he take piano lessons." P. B. Kurland, "Foreword: 'Equal in Origin and Equal in Title to the Legislative Branches of the Government,'" 78 *Harvard Law Review*, 143, 176 (1964).

there are those, but in increasing volume notes that amount to another tune. There is in being a reaction to the steady unification and nationalization of recent years, a movement toward a decentralization and a diversity of which the as yet unacknowledged prophet—due, I should suppose, for a revival—is Brandeis. "The great America for which we long," wrote Brandeis in 1920, "is unattainable unless that individuality of communities becomes far more highly developed and becomes a common American phenomenon. For a century our growth has come through national expansion and the increase of the functions of the Federal Government. The growth of the future—at least of the immediate future—must be in quality and spiritual value. And that can come only through the concentrated, intensified striving of smaller groups. The field of special effort shall now be the State, the city, the village—and each should be led to seek to excel in something peculiar to it. If ideals are developed locally—the national ones will come pretty near to taking care of themselves."[14]

Diversity implies less rather than more law, and certainly less centralized, national law. A striving for diversity is not necessarily in express conflict with the goal of an egalitarian society, but it connotes a different order of priorities. In politics, even as the Warren Court's virtually irresistible slogan—one man, one vote—may still be mouthed on all sides, the cry is for a group participation which presupposes, whether it knows it or not, the Madisonian more than the majoritarian model, and for a process calculated to heed the expression not only of desires and preferences, but of intensities that no ballot can register. These are all indications that the society of the rather near future may be forming beyond the horizon on which the Warren Court's gaze was fixed, that it may be taking on shapes the Court did not perceive and its law cannot accommodate; that, in sum, the society may not be conforming to the Warren Court's vision. This hypothesis should be tested against developments in the public schools, with which the Warren Court was continuously concerned, of course, after *Brown* v. *Board of Education,* and against emerging conditions in the political thicket[15] —to use Justice Frankfurter's famous phrase—which the Court entered with its first apportionment decision in 1962.

The drift of events in the public schools is sufficiently signaled perhaps by the distorted mirror image presented in the Ocean Hill–Brownsville District of New York during the teachers' strikes of the fall of 1968. A decade earlier, black children in Little Rock, Arkansas, and elsewhere in the South were escorted by armed men through unfriendly white crowds to be taught by white teachers. In Ocean Hill–Brownsville in 1968, white teachers had to be escorted by armed men through unfriendly black crowds to teach black children. This was, pray God, an isolated incident, in its own way set apart, much like the Jehovah's Witnesses transfusion cases, by its singularly painful circumstances. But it portends.

At the first argument of *Brown* v. *Board of Education* in 1952, Justice Frankfurter asked the future Justice Thurgood Marshall, then counsel for the Negro children, whether a decision in his favor would "entitle every mother to have her child go to a nonsegregated school?"

Mr. Marshall replied in the negative. "What will it do?" Justice Frankfurter pursued. Mr. Marshall replied: "The school board, I assume, would find some other method of distributing the children by drawing district lines." The only requirement would be, Mr. Marshall added, that the lines be drawn "on a natural basis," and not be gerrymandered so as to enclose or exclude Negro neighborhoods.[16]

It has not been that simple. It has not been that simple because for a decade resistance to any desegregation, of any sort, in any measure, was fierce and uncompromising in much of the South, and even now many districts are yielding only grudgingly, and must still be pushed step by step. It has not been that simple also because the laconic opinion in *Brown* v. *Board of Education* was itself not that simple. One strain in it became evident in subsequent decisions outlawing all forms of state-sponsored segregation in everything from the spectator section of a courtroom to golf courses.[17] The minimal proposition that emerged—and about time it was that it should emerge— was that the state may not, by legislation or administratively, classify the population along racial lines.

As Mr. Wechsler foresaw,[18] this proposition has caused some trouble—not so much in Southern school desegregation cases, where judges, exercising their equity power to exact actual rather than merely nominal compliance with the rule of *Brown* v. *Board of Education,* have ordered school authorities to take remedial measures that, as such, naturally classify pupils by race;[19] but in Northern cases, where racial classifications have been used by local authorities to confer what are regarded as benefits on

Negroes, and the complaining parties have been whites.[20] The Supreme Court itself has regarded these difficulties as transient, and has succeeded in ignoring them.

Another element in the *Brown* decision was the Court's concern, not with race relations in general, but specifically with education. "Today," said the Court in *Brown,* "education is perhaps the most important function of state and local governments. Compulsory school attendance laws and the great expenditures for education both demonstrate our recognition of the importance of education to our democratic society. . . . It is the very foundation of good citizenship." The opportunity for an education, the Court concluded, "where the state has undertaken to provide it," is a right to be made available to all on equal terms. Separate schools did not make it so available because the black child's sense that he was classified by race induced a feeling of inferiority in him, which affected his motivation. The child's education was consequently impaired; it was unequal.

Now it is not easy to maintain the position that the impairment and the inequality result only from segregation imposed by official legislative or administrative action, and not from separation as such, however it may have come about, by official or private initiative, exercised recently or long ago. If a Negro child perceives his separation as discriminatory and invidious, he is not, in a society a hundred years removed from slavery, going to make fine distinctions about the source of a particular separation. The Court implied as much when it quoted with approval a statement by a lower-court judge to the effect that the detrimental consequences of school segregation were heightened—merely heightened—when segregation had the sanction of law.

From here it is a very short step to yet another idea, namely, that separate public schooling, whatever the cause of it, the means by which it is enforced, or its psychological impact on the individual black child, is inherently inferior for everyone concerned, because the function of the public school cannot be successfully performed unless children of all groups are taught in it together. This also the Court implied when it cited certain earlier higher-education cases in which it had held that, quite aside from any psychological impact on the individual Negro student, a school that taught one group in the community in isolation from other groups could not give an adequate professional education. The school, the Court had suggested, is the gateway to the profession, and it could scarcely be an effective gateway if it isolated the student from groups other than his own which constitute the bulk of the profession. Separation in a graduate school, moreover, the Court had said, and now quoted itself in the *Brown* opinion, impaired the student's ability "to engage in discussions and exchange views with other students, and, in general, to learn his profession."

Such considerations, the Court said in *Brown*, "apply with added force to children in grade and high schools," because in children there is generated a feeling of inferiority "that may affect their hearts and minds in a way unlikely ever to be undone."[21] Such considerations apply with added force. They apply first of all with equal force, because for reasons analogous to those that hold in professional schools, but particular to itself, the public school also fails in its mission if it teaches the races separately. That mission, since it cannot be discharged by segregated schools, must be an equalizing, socializing, nationalizing —assimilationist and secular—mission. The implication that the public schools are charged with it stems from the history of public education in the United States—or at least from the history of what men have thought about public education in the United States—and it unites the opinion in *Brown* v. *Board of Education* with the Court's decisions forbidding school prayers and state aid to parochial schools.

Compulsory public schooling in the United States is not much more than a century old. Common schools existed before that, to be sure, but they were extensions of family and church. Yet, even in the early years of the Republic, they took on an equalizing role, the function of opening economic and social opportunity unlimited by background. And as Professor Bernard Bailyn has shown, an assimilationist—civilizing, it was thought—mission was occasionally assigned to education even in the eighteenth century, as intimations of "the problem of group relations in a society of divergent cultures" began to be felt.[22]

The full-blown conception of the public school as a secular, nationalizing, assimilationist agent dates more or less to the post-Civil War years of the great immigrations.[23] In addition to providing rudimentary training for citizenship, and to serving the ideal of upward mobility by equipping the poor as well as the rich with skills—missions that the state could accomplish by supporting and supervising education without providing state-owned and state-managed schools—the public schools were charged with the task of Americanization, of melding backgrounds and creating one nation. Thus the New Haven superintendent of schools said in his annual report of 1919: "The public school is the greatest and most effective of all Americanization agencies. This is the one place where all children in a community or district, regardless of nationality, religion, politics, or social status, meet and work together in a cooperative and harmonious spirit. . . . The children work and play together, they catch the school spirit, they live the democratic life, American heroes become their own, American history wins their loyalty, the Stars and Stripes, always before their eyes in the school room, receives their daily salute. Not only are these immigrant children Americanized through the public school, but they, in turn, Americanize their parents carrying into the home many lessons of democracy learned at school."

Performance of the assimilationist function required government-owned and government-managed schools, the presence in the classroom of children of all nationalities, religions, and classes, and the de-emphasis of factors like religion, which divided rather than united the children. "For their part," says Professor Dahl, describing New Haven, "the immigrants and their children were highly motivated to learn how to be Americans, for they were desperately, sometimes pathetically, eager to win acceptance as true Americans." And: "The result was as astonishing an act of voluntary political and cultural assimilation and speedy elimination of regional, ethnic, and cultural dissimiliarities as history can provide."[24]

Whether, in the large cities at any rate, the process ever

worked quite as thus idealized may be doubted. The mix of nationalities, religions, and social classes was very likely not what the prescription called for. Rather a great deal of homogeneity prevailed in many a school and classroom.[25] But at least earlier arrivals, themselves acculturated, taught the children, and it was clear that assimilation was the goal. In nonracial cases dealing with public and parochial schools, before and after *Brown* v. *Board of Education,* various Justices have stressed this goal, often defining it more explicitly than the Court did in *Brown.*

Justice Frankfurter, of course, viewed the flag salute as no less significant than it had seemed to the superintendent of the New Haven public schools in 1919, and as significant for exactly the same reason.* And, concurring in a decision that a released-time program for religious instruction of public-school pupils was unconstitutional, Frankfurter said: "Designed to serve as perhaps the most powerful agency for promoting cohesion among a heterogeneous democratic people, the public school must keep scrupulously free from entanglement in the strife of sects." The public school he said was "at once the symbol of our democracy and the most pervasive means for promoting our common destiny."[26] Justice Brennan for his part wrote as follows in support of the Warren Court's decision that religious prayer of any sort, however nondenominational and even innocuous, is unconstitutional in the public schools: "Whatever Jefferson or Madison would have thought of Bible reading or the recital of the Lord's Prayer in what few public schools existed in their

* See *supra,* p. 33.

day . . . the American experiment in free public education" has evolved to the point where the schools now "serve a uniquely *public* function: the training of American citizens in an atmosphere free of parochial, divisive, or separatist influences of any sort—an atmosphere in which children may assimilate a heritage common to all American groups and religions."[27]

The mission of the public school so conceived would have required not only compulsory free public education, but exclusive compulsory free public education. In the xenophobic period following World War I, this logic began to take hold. Oregon in effect forbade attendance at private schools by normal children who had not completed the eighth grade. But the Court intervened, as we have seen.[*] To go this far, it said, was unreasonably to interfere "with the liberty of parents and guardians to direct the upbringing and education of children under their control. . . . The fundamental theory of liberty upon which all governments in this Union repose excludes any general power of the State to standardize its children by forcing them to accept instruction from public teachers only. The child is not the mere creature of the State; those who nurture him and direct his destiny have the right, coupled with the high duty, to recognize and prepare him for additional obligations."[28]

The ability of the public schools to perform their mission would have to be ensured only by their highly favorable competitive position. That position, in turn, rested on the Court's construction of the First Amendment's Estab-

[*] See *supra,* p. 25.

lishment of Religion Clause as forbidding state support of church-connected private schools, which is what most private schools are. "No tax in any amount, large or small, can be levied to support any religious activities or institutions, whatever they may be called, or whatever form they may adopt to teach or practice religion." So said the Court in *Everson* v. *Board of Education*,[29] even while it was slightly eroding the public schools' competitive position by allowing public busing for parochial-school pupils.

The Warren Court further eroded the position somewhat by holding generally—although reserving judgment on specific instances—that a state may lend textbooks free of charge to parochial students, even though, as the Court said, free books may perhaps "make it more likely that some children choose to attend a sectarian school."[30] But, on the whole, the competitive position of the public schools continues strong, and reliance on it as ensuring ability to perform the nationalizing mission is not misplaced. It remains a gross overstatement to say, as Justice Brennan has done, that the First Amendment forbids the state "to inhibit" the individual's choice "between a public secular education with its uniquely democratic values, and some form of private or sectarian education, which offers values of its own."[31] The public schools are free, supported by public funds to which everyone, including parochial-school parents, contributes their taxes; private schools still have little if any access to public funds, and must be supported out of private pockets.*

---

* Another aspect of the accommodation is a measure of control by the state over the indoctrination administered to its future citizens in private schools. "No question is raised," said the Court in Pierce

For a decade, the conception of the function of public schools implicit in *Brown* v. *Board of Education,* and the relationship between *Brown* and the law of other school cases had no bearing on the process of administering the desegregation of Southern schools. Much of the South challenged the minimal requirement of *Brown:* that segregation cease being enforced by law. Making at times dramatic use of their equity powers, the lower federal courts, with the exception of certain unsympathetic and even rebellious judges,[32] but with the support of the Supreme Court, withstood this challenge in its many shapes.[33] (In 1964, in the Civil Rights Act of that year, Congress came to the aid of the courts by giving legislative form to the minimal rule of the *Brown* case, and

---

v. Society of Sisters, *supra* n. 28, 268 U.S. at 534; and see Board of Education v. Allen, *supra* n. 30, 392 U.S. at 246–47, "concerning the power of the state reasonably to regulate all schools, to inspect, supervise and examine them, their teachers and pupils; to require that all children of proper age attend some school, that teachers shall be of good moral character and patriotic disposition, that certain studies plainly essential to good citizenship must be taught, and that nothing be taught which is manifestly inimical to the public welfare." But here too there are limits. The state may not forbid the teaching of foreign languages. Meyer v. Nebraska, 262 U.S. 390 (1923); Bartels v. Iowa, 262 U.S. 404 (1923). Even in its public schools it may not forbid the teaching of so conventional and established an aspect of Western intellectual history as the Darwinian theory, at least when the Court surmises that the prohibition is motivated by a counter-theory that is religious in nature; and perhaps the state could not forbid the teaching of other well-established hypotheses. Epperson v. Arkansas, 393 U.S. 97 (1968). And the state is limited by the First Amendment in the measures it can take, in the public schools, let alone in private ones, to ensure that teachers are "of good moral character and patriotic disposition." See, *e.g.,* Whitehill v. Elkins, 389 U.S. 54 (1967).

putting additional if very limited resources into its enforcement.)[34]

When schools were closed by state authorities for the sole reason that federal courts had ordered them desegregated, the actions were held unconstitutional, and the schools in effect reopened by court decree.[35] When state and local governments, as part of the same statutory schemes that closed public schools in order to prevent their desegregation, made available tuition grants to pupils transferring to segregated private schools, so-called, the payment of the tuition grants was forbidden—although it was somewhat curious that the courts should forbid payment of the grants rather than order the desegregation of the private schools, which they found to be thinly disguised substitutes for segregated public schools.[36]

In the second decade of desegregation, the totally unyielding resistance of earlier years having been broken for the most part,* the minimal rule of *Brown* took on some complexity, and the Warren Court's assumptions concern-

---

* Pockets of recalcitrance remain. Resistance is more ingenious now than blatant, but often effective. Overall figures for the eleven Southern states in 1968–69 showed progress: 20.3 percent of Negro children attending school with whites. But in the more resistant states the figure was much lower: 7.4 percent in Alabama, 7.1 in Mississippi. See *New York Times,* February 23, 1969, p. 51, col. 3. Some judges issue tough decrees, others do not, and those who do are in a poor position to monitor compliance. Insufficient resources and personnel have been committed to the enforcement of orders issued by the Department of Health, Education and Welfare under the Civil Rights Act of 1964. The courts and the Department have generally cooperated, but sometimes they trip over each other's feet. See Lee v. Macon County Board of Education, 270 F. Supp. 859 (M.D. Ala. 1967); and see Lee v. Macon County Board of Education, 292 F. Supp. 363 (M.D. Ala. 1968).

ing the effect of segregation on the Negro child, and concerning the necessary role of public schools began to come into play, however indirectly.

The courts have been faced with token compliance, and with devices calculated to enable school boards to retain as many segregated situations as possible. Like the Department of Health, Education and Welfare in its own efforts to implement the Civil Rights Act of 1964, the courts have sometimes responded with orders that Southern school boards produce a given percentage of Negro children in desegregated schools by a given date.[37] And since a segregated faculty characterizes a school as white or Negro, faculties have also been required to be integrated on a percentage basis.[38]

In a series of cases decided in May, 1968, the Supreme Court said that Southern school boards must produce desegregation plans that work realistically, and "work *now.*" A plan that works, the Court made fairly clear, is a plan that does not merely free Negro children to attend white schools, but that actually results in integrated schools *now.* The Court held that in a rural district, with relatively little housing segregation, a freedom-of-choice plan, under which all pupils, white and Negro, could choose which school to attend, had not worked satisfactorily. The plan had produced not a single white child attending the formerly all-Negro school, although 115 Negro children enrolled in the formerly all-white school. Eighty-five percent of the Negro children in the district remained in the all-Negro school.

The Court's holding was tied to evidence of foot dragging and bad faith on the part of the school board. A freedom-of-choice plan implemented in good faith was not necessarily unconstitutional, the Court said, taking account, for once, of varied conditions, and tolerating some diversity. But where other courses of action, promising more desegregation, are open to the board, the Court went on, failure to take them "may indicate a lack of good faith; and at the least it places a heavy burden upon the board to explain its preference for an apparently less effective method." The Court added even more explicitly that "if there are reasonably available other ways, such for illustration as zoning, promising speedier and more effective conversion to a unitary, non-racial school system, 'freedom of choice' must be held unacceptable."[39]

Another of the cases decided by the Supreme Court in May, 1968, arose in Jackson, Tennessee, a city of forty thousand with a school population some 40 percent Negro, which put a nonracial zoning plan into effect, but allowed free transfers of students out of their zones, limited only by the availability of space elsewhere. The result was that all whites assigned to previously Negro schools transferred out, and many Negroes transferred back to Negro schools after being assigned to previously all-white ones. Schools that were previously all-Negro remained so, even though one junior high school was fairly thoroughly integrated, as were also one or two elementary schools. The Court held that this performance was "clearly inadequate," and that the transfers must cease. But again the holding was tied to intimations of the school board's bad faith.[40]

Shortly after, the Court of Appeals for the Fifth Circuit upheld an order to the Jacksonville, Florida, board of education, which had desegregated with a plan quite like that of Jackson, Tennessee, not only to discontinue free transfers that were resegregating schools in some zones, but to permit transfers of students from schools where they were in a racial majority to other schools where they would be in a racial minority.[41] An occasional lower federal court in the South has also enjoined the construction of a new school on a site that would tend to entrench segregation rather than being likely to conduce to integration, or the rehabilitation of a previously *de jure* and now *de facto* Negro school, which might have the same effect.[42]

Only in some cities have Southern conditions quite come to resemble the situation in the North and West, where there is generally no problem of segregation imposed by law. Hence, decrees in cases such as those just discussed do not in theory rest on the proposition that any sort of segregation, however arrived at, hurts the Negro child, is also otherwise inconsistent with the mission of the public schools, and is for these reasons unconstitutional; and these decrees do not expressly require racial balance in the schools. Rather, against a background of sustained resistance, they purport merely to demand the production of convincing evidence of compliance with the minimal rule that legally-imposed segregation must be disestablished. Yet, even if only for evidentiary purposes, these decrees also require more than just disestablishment, and they reflect, therefore, all the elements that entered into the decision of *Brown* v. *Board of Education*, not simply the rule that state-sponsored segregation is unconstitutional. On their face, they are informed by a conception of the mission of the public school as assimilationist—a conception that is as pertinent to the rest of the country as to the South.

Outside the South, of course, school segregation is massive, and has, indeed, increased substantially in recent years, even though it has not been established by law for many decades, but is caused mainly by residential patterns.[43] Nevertheless, very few federal courts have tried to intervene, none has done so without qualification, and the Supreme Court has carefully refrained from becoming involved.[44] Here and there, school authorities have been shown to have intentionally instituted or fostered segregation,[45] and perhaps that could be shown more often than it has been.[46] Where it has been, federal courts have issued decrees somewhat like the ones in the latest, most advanced Southern cases, but seldom otherwise.

The reasons for caution outside the South are not far to seek. If a court has been teasing and dragging a resistant or even a reluctant school board away from a policy of legally enforced segregation, and that school board declines to put into effect a neighborhood school policy, or allows a certain kind of transfer of pupils out of neighborhood schools but does not permit another kind, or chooses a certain site for a new school rather than another one, or puts a rigid track system into effect, or improves a certain school instead of closing it, a judge who arrives at the conclusion that alternate policies would result in more integration is entitled to believe that the school board's own choice of policies was not based entirely on educational or other neutral criteria. He may, therefore, feel reasonably confident in reversing that choice to the end of ultimately conducing to a racially neutral pursuit of edu-

131

cational policy by a school board, without hidden racial motives or mental reservations. This judicial posture is possible in most districts in the South, and it is possible elsewhere, if a finding of recent intentional segregation, as by the gerrymandering of school districts, can be made.

When, however, there is no reason to take the basic assumption of bad faith or of a mental reservation in favor of a segregated system, then a judge who is asked to modify decisions about districting, or site selection, or tracking of pupils, or failure to bus, or failure to close a school, or failure to pair two schools, or to consolidate one or more grades in a central school—a judge asked to review and reverse such decisions is then in a position of simply remaking educational and other local policy. He must either be able to convince himself that the goal of integration overrides all others and that the schools must discharge their assimiliationist mission at all costs, regardless of other considerations, or he must have uncommon confidence in his own capacity as an educational policy maker.

But that is not the worst of it. In most of the larger urban areas, demographic conditions are such that no policy that a court can order, and a school board, a city, or even a state has the capability to put into effect, will in fact result in the foreseeable future in racially balanced public schools. Only a reordering of the environment involving economic and social policy on the broadest conceivable front might have an appreciable impact. Judges have, therefore, felt relatively helpless, and reluctant to hold out promises that the law could not redeem.

The intractability of the problem in large and medium

cities has consequences also for smaller urban communities, in which demographic conditions might more readily permit some dispersal of racial groups through the school system. For it is one thing to tell district judges in the South, as the Warren Court did, that no single rule of thumb exists concerning methods of desegregation, and that different conditions might make different methods appropriate in various communities. It is one thing also, as the Court too seldom did, to withhold centralized national law, and allow private institutions or local governments to evolve diverse policies. Diversity of school policies exists now, pursuant to the play of state and local initiative. A number of communities are making their own efforts to achieve better racial balance in their schools.[47] It is quite another thing, however, to issue, out of the same federal judiciary, one binding rule of constitutional law for Manhasset, New York, let us say (*de facto* segregation is unconstitutional and measures, such as school pairing and busing and transfer plans, must be taken to balance the races in the schools), and a different rule of constitutional law for New York City (*de facto* segregation is inevitable and hence not unconstitutional).

The predicament of unequal application of national law will, incidentally, be arrived at in the South if freedom-of-choice plans are forbidden, and school zoning is ordered in rural districts that do not have residential segregation, and yet zoning is allowed to produce massive *de facto* segregation in Southern cities as in Northern ones. The result will be seen as an unequal application of law, as an encouragement of residential segregation, and as the imposition of a cost on residential dispersal—all from the point of view, of course, of communities reluctant to mix races in the schools.

Present judicial attitudes toward *de facto* segregation are not stable. All too many federal judges have been induced to view themselves as holding roving commissions as problem solvers, and as charged with a duty to act when majoritarian institutions do not. Not all of them have so far resisted, and not all will resist, invitations to take charge, whether by being more skeptical of the *bona fides* of local school administrators, or by directly confronting the *de facto* problem. Even the triviality of the results that are achievable in medium and large cities[48] may not deter some judges. And the inevitable consequence of judicial interventions, as of local and legislative initiatives, to alleviate racial isolation in the public schools must be the centralization of school administration. For, given the geographic concentration of Negroes in neighborhoods and very nearly in whole cities, enlargement of the administrative jurisdiction offers the only hope of alleviation.

The same tendency toward central control of schools is indicated by the only available theoretical justification—such as it is—for applying unequal law as between smaller and larger urban communities, or law with different consequences as between rural and urban communities in the South. This justification, formulated in an influential article by Professor Owen Fi 49 is used in one of the Supreme Court's recent Sout rn cases, noted above.° It is that while there cannot be a constitutional

° See *supra,* pp. 128–29.

duty to perform the impossible, there is a duty, when alternate feasible policies of school location and of pupil assignment are open to the authorities, to adopt that policy which will lead to more rather than less integration. Seen from the vantage point of a local school board, this may mean a school pairing here, a transfer plan there. But a duty rests on the state also,[50] and seen from its vantage point, the theory means consolidation of school districts, long-range transportation, educational parks, in short, central management. And since the federal government is under an obligation to spend its money in conformance with constitutional requirements—no more than a state may the federal government give financial support to segregated institutions—the theory necessarily means that the federal government has a duty to impose policies leading to integration, if it continues any financial support of schools.

It is thus quite evident that unless *Brown* v. *Board of Education* is restricted to the general proposition that segregation enforced by law is unconstitutional, and is denuded of any policy relating specifically to schools, it must bring on a dramatic centralization of control over the public schools. Efforts, now afoot, to equalize on a statewide basis disparate local expenditures for public schooling are also likely to tend in a centralizing direction—indeed, perhaps in a nationalizing direction, since if state expenditures are constitutionally equalized, it will become increasingly difficult to support the proposition that Mississippi may continue to spend half or a third as much as New York and California on its public-school pupils. The equalization efforts, aimed ultimately at recapturing and redistributing school funds that are raised locally, have been unavailing in the federal courts, but they may attain legislative success.[51]

The centralization can come readily enough, and given an infusion of fresh federal funds, so can some measure of equalization of expenditures.[52] But whether significant integration can be achieved even under centralized control is quite another question. The situation is complicated by the accommodation reached long ago in *Pierce* v. *Society of Sisters*—the compromise, if you will, with the ideal of the public school as an assimilationist, egalitarian agency.* For whites within integrating range are fleeing to private schools, parochial and otherwise.

"We are frankly told in the Brief," noted the Supreme Court in the Jackson, Tennessee, case mentioned earlier, "that without the transfer option [which the Court forbade] . . . white students will flee the school system altogether." The Court's answer, in the language of *Brown* v. *Board of Education* itself, was that "it should go without saying that the vitality of these constitutional principles cannot be allowed to yield simply because of disagreement with them."[53] But their intended effect may have to yield to reality, whether their theoretical vitality is allowed to or not.

Shall the escape route of *Pierce* v. *Society of Sisters* be closed off? Even if it should be, there are numerous whites who without resorting to private schools retain the option —which most assuredly is not going to be denied them— of moving out of range, if not of centralized school au-

* See *supra*, p. 124.

thorities altogether, then of the means of integration available to them. There are private public schools, as they have been called, in many a suburb, and even heroic centralization of control and statewide or national equalization of expenditures will not soon change their nature. The upshot, then, of judicial action against *de facto* segregation would be that an integrated education, if any, is willy-nilly for the poor, but a matter of choice for the well-to-do, even as now centrally and remotely administered schools are for the poor, but the well-to-do community can control its own schools. And an education rigorously devoid of any religious—or, as some would say, moral—content is willy-nilly for the poor, but more a matter of choice for the well-to-do. The well-to-do are defined both in personal and in group terms: the individual well-to-do in some suburban and in private schools, and groups that are backed by an ancient and strong institution, in parochial schools.

These consequences hardly square with the nationalizing, egalitarian, assimilationist conception of the public schools' mission. They hardly square either with what little is known to substantiate the assumption of *Brown* v. *Board of Education* that a segregated education hurts the Negro child. For it appears that segregation by socio-economic class more than by race may affect the quality of education for the individual child. Hence a racially integrated but socio-economically homogeneous school may, so far as one can tell, be damaging to the educational process, if anything in the school, as opposed to the home environment, is.[54] And so the law may find itself straining to attain conditions in the public schools that serve no known purpose by way of educational benefit to the child, strictly speaking, and that do not further performance of the egalitarian, assimilationist mission of the schools. At the same time, the law would be producing a most unequal result as between poor and well-to-do parents, and between institutionally-supported groups in the society and newer, less established ones. A strange destination for the most egalitarian of Courts to arrive at!

People closest to the reality of things are discovering that this is indeed the destination toward which the egalitarian and assimilationist presuppositions of judicial decisions are propelling the constitutional law of public schools. At the same time, the assimilationist objective is far from universally shared—in the middle class, or in the principal group, the Negroes, that remains to be assimilated.[55] Even if desirable, the ideal seems, as the public schools pursue it, increasingly illusory and myth-ridden. And, if desirable, it seems sufficiently—perhaps too well—served by other agencies in the society, using modern techniques of communication and indoctrination.

What scientific evidence there is suggesting that even a school with the ideal mix of social classes and of the races would help Negroes and the poor to achieve upward mobility is sketchy and uncertain.[56] Large, centrally administered school systems, which alone could provide schools with the ideal mix, are—or are seen by many groups, particularly Negroes, as being—more and more sluggish, unresponsive, oppressive; and are in any event failing to provide numerous lower-class children with basic skills. There is renewed emphasis, therefore, on the other aspect of the tradition of American education, the aspect highlighted in *Pierce* v. *Society of Sisters*, in which the Court recognized the indefeasible right of the family to nurture the child and "direct his destiny."

The British-American Protestant, wrote Professor George K. Gardner of Harvard Law School, commenting on *Brown* v. *Board of Education* in 1955, "finds his home invaded by radio and television and his children drawn off to great schools of unprecedented magnitude and efficiency, conducted by a new caste of 'educators,' who seem every year to absorb a larger share of his income, and to play a larger part in the direction of his children's lives." Of course the state ought not classify people by race in its laws, Gardner believed, and ought not decree their segregation. We seek in our schools, however, Gardner protested, "the equality, not of the melting pot, but of the self-directed home."[57]

He was an unheard voice in 1955, drowned in the babble of racists. But although the efficiency he attributed to the schools of great magnitude would no longer be generally conceded, the note he sounded is now heard from groups other than the Catholics and the white Anglo-Saxon Protestants; it is heard from groups that, having seen how Catholics and other whites are able to impose the wishes of the self-directed household on many a suburban public school, and of course on private schools, wish to try the same privilege on for size. Much Negro opinion is now, like Gardner, more intent on group autonomy than on individual equality, or at any rate, realistically, on the equality of autonomous groups first.

Proposals answering to the revived desire that the school be less a creature of the state and its law, and more an extension of the self-directed home range from decentralization plans to tuition-grant schemes. Following a recommendation of the New York City Board of Education, the New York legislature in 1969 subdivided the city's school system into at least thirty community districts, with a student population as small as 20,000 each, though no smaller.[58] These districts approximate the school system of a medium city, such as, for example, New Haven, Connecticut, which is hardly parent-controlled. But most New York districts will likely be quite homogeneous, and in each there will be a locally-elected board. The sense of community and the degree of responsiveness to parents are apt to be at least initially greater than is found in New Haven. The legislation enacted in 1969 gives the local boards all too little direct and specific power over curriculum and teachers, and the sense of community may in these circumstances wither. If it is sustained, however, more power may be expected to flow to the local boards.

A tuition-grant scheme was put forward in 1955 by Professor Gardner, who urged that the state "credit each child of school age with a fixed sum of money, and permit . . . the child's parents to apply this money to the support of a school of their own choice."[59] Professor Milton Friedman has since elaborated this proposal.[60] Properly amended to provide, as others have suggested, for graduated tuition grants, quite high for poor families, and reduced to zero for middle- and high-income ones, this proposal can also in the simplest, least problematic fashion go far to equalize the expenditure of resources for

140

education.[61] It can, at a minimum, be as egalitarian as the progressive income tax.*

Decentralization schemes like New York City's, which retain the public school as such, have already received strong support from virtually all segments of Negro opinion. Even in litigation, where this sort of thing is apt to manifest itself last, an impatience on the part of some Negro groups, although to be sure not all, with integration palliatives has begun to exhibit itself.[62] Tuition plans, in combination with the continued existence of some public schools, or as an ultimate goal implying the abandonment of public schools, may also commend themselves to Negro groups, as they undoubtedly will to parochial-school parents.[63] A body of law, flowing naturally out of *Brown* v. *Board of Education* broadly conceived, will bar the way, however, unless substantially modified or abandoned.

We noted earlier† a series of school-closing cases in the

* The views of Gardner and Friedman are derived from John Stuart Mill, who insisted on egalitarianism. "If the government would make up its mind to *require* for every child a good education," wrote Mill, "it might save itself the trouble of *providing* one. It might leave to parents to obtain the education where and how they pleased, and content itself with helping to pay the school fees of the poorer class of children, and defraying the entire school expenses of those who have no one else to pay for them. . . . A general State education is a mere contrivance for moulding people to be exactly like one another. . . . It establishes a despotism over the mind. . . . An education established and controlled by the State should only exist, if it exists at all, as one among many competing experiments, carried on for the purpose of example and stimulus, to keep the others up to a certain standard of excellence," J. S. Mill, *On Liberty* 129–30 (Oxford World's Classics ed. 1952).
† See *supra*, p. 127.

South in which the act of closing the schools, always selective, was by the plainest and most unmistakable evidence part of a strategy for maintaining segregation. For this reason, the courts, including in the *Prince Edward County* case the Supreme Court, ordered the schools reopened. Tuition plans that were tied entirely to school closings of this ilk, and were meant to tide whites over in temporary quasi-public schools until the segregated situation could be restored in the regular ones, were also struck down.

After massive resistance to desegregation in any form was broken, however, a number of Southern states enacted tuition-grant statutes that could no longer be viewed quite so plainly as part of an effort to continue segregation in the public schools. The question now, formally, was of the reach of constitutional law, and of the nature and extent of private ordering to which the law of the Constitution is not applicable, and which is not subject to supervision and regulation by the federal courts. More fundamentally and ultimately, these latter-day Southern tuition-grant statutes tested the accommodation embodied in *Pierce* v. *Society of Sisters;* they searched the degree to which the federal courts would insist on the assimilationist mission of public schools, would insist that a right to an education, such as Brandeis and Frankfurter regarded as fundamental in their conversation in the 1920's, amounts to an obligation to submit to a public-school education.

Seeking a middle ground, a federal court in Virginia in 1965 held that tuition-grant statutes were not unconstitutional as such, and that any given tuition payment to a parent for use in a private school was "legal if it does not tend in a determinative degree to perpetuate segregation." The test was not the policy of the school in which the tuition grant was used—the school could be segregated— "but the measure in which the grant or grants contribute to effect the exclusion on account of race." It was the part played by aggregate tuition grants in supporting the school that was "pivotal." If the aggregate grants received under the tuition statute "only insubstantially contributed to the running of the school," that school would not be considered to be in effect public and subject to the constitutional command to desegregate, and the payment of tuition grants to individual parents sending their children to it would be unobjectionable. On the other hand, if the aggregate of tuition grants preponderantly maintained the school, then the conclusion would be that the state was nurturing whatever policy that school pursued, including a policy of segregation, and the grants would be held unconstitutional.

This attempt at finding a middle ground was not free from difficulty. If the conclusion was that a school preponderantly supported by public funds was in effect public, why should the consequence not have been an order that it desegregate, rather than an order stopping the payment to it of tuition grants? Yet the court issued a decree forbidding the payment of grants for attendance at a number of schools in Virginia.[64] Moreover, the decision raised questions about other programs, in being or projected, such as tuition payments under the G.I. Bill of Rights, or the National Defense Education Act of 1958, which might substantially support a school, or at least

143

certain activities in it, and even about welfare payments, which in the aggregate may support, as they are spent by the recipients, private housing or some other private activity. In any event, matters did not rest there.

Louisiana, which also had a tutition-grant program, heeded the test propounded by the Virginia court, and administered its statute in conformance with it. It provided administratively that tuition grants would not be paid to applicants whose children "attend any private school predominantly maintained through such tuition grants," and in turn construed this provision as meaning that no tuition grants would be paid which in the aggregate amounted to 50 percent or more of a school's annual operating cost. In *Poindexter* v. *Louisiana Financial Assistance Commission*,[65] a federal court declared this tuition statute, as so administered, unconstitutional, and the Supreme Court, albeit without opinion, affirmed.[66] The *Poindexter* decision placed much reliance in an earlier case, *Hall* v. *St. Helena Parish School Board,* which had dealt with a tuition-grant statute tied, as the court viewed it, to school closings intended to perpetuate public-school segregation, but which had broached a broader proposition, too, and which the Supreme Court had also affirmed.[67]

The *St. Helena Parish* case involved a statutory scheme under which any parish was allowed to exercise local option, hold an election on the question of closing its public-school system, and close it if a majority of voters so wished. Even though the evidence it used was somewhat weak, the court regarded this exercise of local option as indistinguishable from earlier selective closings of schools for the express purpose of preventing their desegregation, and on the well-settled authority of the earlier selective-closing cases, it ordered that the schools remain open. The local-option scheme had a tuition-grant statute attached to it, which the court disposed of at the same time, in the same fashion.

Quite separately, however, the court went on to indicate also that local option concerning school closing was unconstitutional anyway, in itself, regardless of motive. Yet local option applicable to any number of subjects is a standard method of decentralizing state government. Like home rule, it is not generally unconstitutional; it is not held to deny equal protection to one part of the state as against another.[68] Even more significantly, the selective abandonment by a unit of government of functions other than schooling, such as maintenance of public swimming pools, has also been upheld, even against a background of their required desegregation if they were to be retained as public functions.[69] The inference is irresistible, therefore, that the unspoken premise of the court's holding in the *St. Helena Parish* case was that public education is a function the state may not abandon, selectively or altogether. It is in this sense that one should read the court's statement that "grants-in-aid, no matter how generous, are not an adequate substitute for public schools."[70] The court went on to refer to organizational and administrative advantages and economies that would be lost to a school system not operating under the aegis of the state. Yet surely the voters of any region are free to deprecate the mere administrative advantages of a centralized school system; they can hardly be under a federal constitutional obligation to avail themselves of administrative advantages.

The *St. Helena Parish* opinion is notable also for the court's finding of continued state involvement with projected private schools in which tuition grants might be used. The court detected the hand of the state—which would render the projected private schools public in contemplation of law—in provisions for school lunches and transportation to be made available to private schools, and provisions to secure the tenure of teachers formerly in the public system who took employment in the private schools, and to protect their salary structure and that of other school workers. It is of far-reaching importance that the court saw in these provisions a state interest sufficient to render private schools to which they applied effectively public, because they are provisions that are bound to be typical of any transition from a system of full public schooling to a system, however partial, of some privately-operated schools supported through tuition grants. It is hard to imagine the possibility of any transition in the absence of some provisions such as these.

The Supreme Court affirmed the *St. Helena Parish* case without comment, but in referring to it later in its own opinion in the *Prince Edward County*° case, it characterized it in the narrow terms of earlier school-closing decisions, without reference to the broader ground also taken by the lower court. And in its *Prince Edward County* opinion the Court pointed out the general validity of home-rule and local-option arrangements. Yet the *Poin-*

° See *supra*, p. 127, n. 35.

dexter case, which was also affirmed without comment, and which came after *Prince Edward,* occupies the broad ground tentatively entered upon in *Hall* v. *St. Helena Parish.* Indeed it takes even broader ground.

Louisiana now was no longer attempting to close any public schools. It was merely trying to support alternatives to them also. On the obvious if tacit assumption that the maintenance, not merely of public schools, but of their favored competitive position is a constitutional duty of the state, the court went so far as to suggest that in the circumstances of Louisiana, any encouragement by the state of private schools will conduce to the continued segregation, or the resegregation, of public schools, because it will draw middle-class whites out of the public schools; and that for this reason alone state support of private schools by means of tuition grants is unconstitutional.

Most recently, reversing its own earlier partial approval of some uses of the Virginia tuition plan, a federal court has read the Supreme Court's affirmance of the *Poindexter* case, and of a similar decision in South Carolina,[71] as meaning that the validity of a tuition plan depends on "whether the arrangement in *any* measure, no matter how slight, contributes to or permits continuance of segregated public school education. This pronouncement is uncompromisingly dictated in the [Supreme] Court's approval of the decrees striking down the tuition grant laws of Louisiana and South Carolina. . . . In our judgment, it follows, that neither motive nor purpose is an indispensable element of the breach. The *effect* of the State's

147

contribution is a sufficient determinant, with effect ascertained entirely objectively."[72]

The effect, always and everywhere, is to contribute to the segregation of public schools. The difference, moreover, between a state statute that encourages private schools by making tuition grants available and a state statute that merely permits the requirement of schooling to be fulfilled in private schools, which in turn it regulates for compliance with curricular and other standards—the difference is that the one extends to the poor a privilege made available by the other to the well-to-do. Both kinds of statutes encourage and support private schools. And both kinds of private schools, in the North as well as in the South, conduce substantially to the continued segregation or the resegregation of the public schools, since both draw out the middle class. Yet the Court in the *Poindexter* case purported not in any measure to be disturbing the continued validity of *Pierce* v. *Society of Sisters!*

The result the courts have reached is hardly sustainable. It confirms and further entrenches the unequal system of private or public, parent-controlled schools for well-to-do, mobile whites, and state-controlled, assimilationist schools for the white and black poor; and it forbids the state to alleviate the inequality. In *Coppedge* v. *Franklin County Board of Education,* a Southern case, Negro children involuntarily transferred to a formerly all-white school intervened, asking the court to permit them to remain in the all-Negro school. The court would have none of this. The Constitution, it said, commands not free individual choice, but desegregation—achievable in this particular North Carolina county only by geographical zoning of the schools.[73] That is all very well, but can anyone offer assurance that the problems of schooling, and more generally of relations between the races, are soluble only in accordance with present judicial prescriptions, regardless of the perverse and increasingly unwanted results they achieve, and that other solutions or transitional expedients are not worth trying?

Under pressure, the insistence on the assimilationist mission of public schools which are unable to perform it cannot be maintained, and it should not be. When it is abandoned, decisions forbidding religious exercises in the schools, or financial support by the state to church-connected schools must also go. To attach the law of the Constitution to tuition grants, and hold that private schools predominantly supported by grants are in effect public and may not sponsor religious exercises would defeat the essence of the policy of a tuition-grant scheme. The Constitution, moreover, not only forbids "an establishment of religion," but also guarantees "the free exercise thereof." Prayer in private schools some of whose pupils draw public money has more the look of free exercise than of establishment.[74] If schools supported by the state in indirect fashion may sponsor religious exercises, what good reason would there be for holding that schools directly financed by the state, but relegated to parent and community control, may not?[75]

Again, if tuition grants are generally available, will it be possible to withhold them from children wishing to attend parochial schools? In theory perhaps, and the Southern tuition-grant statutes that have been declared unconstitutional forbade attendance at church-related schools. But in many another state, the discrimination is politically unthinkable, and otherwise not readily tenable. And if the state may indirectly supply general-purpose financial support to a church-connected school through tuition grants, why may it not do so by means of direct payments to the school itself? The state should not favor one sect over another, or religious education over secular, but that is a very different matter. The position now is that it must favor secular over religious education.

No doubt, schools and any other institutions mainly supported by tuition grants may and should still be held subject to the minimal rule of *Brown* v. *Board of Education,* which forbids state-enforced or state-sponsored segregation. An appreciable number will in fact be integrated, as many private schools are now. Yet assuredly many private schools, as also many decentralized public schools, would be *de facto* segregated, or nearly so.

We cannot, said the Court in *Brown* v. *Board of Education,* "turn the clock back to 1868 when the [Fourteenth] Amendment was adopted, or even to 1896 when *Plessy* v. *Ferguson* was written. We must consider public education in light of its full development and its present place in American life throughout the Nation."[76] That development, we now know, was not full and not final at the time of *Brown,* and that place is changing. What the *Brown* opinion ultimately envisioned seems for the moment unattainable, and is becoming unwanted. Soon it may be impossible to "turn the clock back" to 1954, when *Brown* v. *Board of Education* was written. This is not to detract from the nobility of the Warren Court's aspiration

150

in *Brown,* nor from the contribution to American life of the rule that the state may not coerce or enforce the separation of the races. But it is to say that *Brown* v. *Board of Education,* with emphasis on the education part of the title, may be headed for—dread word—irrelevance.

An even unkinder fate awaits the one-man, one-vote rule of the Warren Court's legislative apportionment cases. Similar junctures have been reached in apportionment and school controversies. In the school cases, the Court, inevitably enough, pushed from its initial deliberate-speed formula to the requirement that desegregation be accomplished by devices that work visibly, significantly, and now. So in apportionment cases, having started with the demand that legislative districts be "as nearly of equal population as is practicable,"[77] the Court has ended by insisting on mathematical equality.[78]

Exact equality of districts was always in fact practicable, just as reasonably immediate desegregation without deliberate speed was always possible. Both of the Court's qualifying formulas were a recognition, not that administrative factors would necessarily cause delay, but that resistance might do so. It did and does in school desegregation, but it hardly did and scarcely does in re-apportionment. Much sooner, therefore, than with the schools, the Court in apportionment cases now confronts issues that are more complex and ramified by several orders of magnitude; issues that stand in relation to the question presented in the first reapportionment case of 1962 as *de facto* school segregation stands to *de jure.*

Given that districts are to be equal, the question is, what is a proper constituency, a proper district? A legislative or other constituency that is thought to be improper even though equal, because it favors one group or interest over another, is called gerrymandered. The Court has said that the majority must rule. Now the question is, which majority? If a method of districting turns what should have been a majority into a minority, it defeats the Court's principle and is unacceptable. The rub is that virtually all districting turns what might have been a majority into a minority.*

Moreover, even if districting is accepted as enabling a true majority to rule, and especially if distortions of the true majority are corrected by enlarging the constituency, should not the minority have some representation also? If so, the puzzle of the proper district is back again, only from another perspective. And if minorities deserve representation, are they also entitled to a measure of effective power, or must the Court forbid such counter-majoritarian practices as the requirement of a two-thirds

---

* In Wells v. Rockefeller, *infra* n. 88, the Court held that New York's 1968 Congressional apportionment was constitutionally deficient in that it created districts that were not exactly equal. (There was a claim that the apportionment was a systematic partisan gerrymander, but the Court found it unnecessary to deal with this issue.) The upshot was that the New York legislature was required to reapportion once more, and to produce more perfectly equal districts, so to speak. A high-ranking Republican in New York, noting that his party was in control of the legislature, rejoiced. "Now it's just a question of slicing the salami," he told a reporter, "and the salami happens to be in our hands. I think we will have a Republican majority from New York in the House in the 1970 elections. We can draw beautiful lines that can be as compact as a good cigar and still achieve a switch of six to eight seats for our side." *New York Times*, April 8, 1969, p. 34, col. 3 ("State Republicans See a Gain of 6 to 8 House Seats").

legislative vote, or of a constitutional amendment, for some purposes? By indirection, as we have seen, in *Reitman* v. *Mulkey* and in its sequel, *Hunter* v. *Erickson,* the Court has already thrown certain of these practices into doubt.*

These issues have been in view from the beginning; they were not, like *de facto* segregation at the time of *Brown* v. *Board of Education,* dimly foreseeable and due to be aggravated and brought to the fore by changes in demographic conditions.[79] Nor, again unlike *de facto* segregation, are these issues basically novel to the experience of the Court, except in the multitude of forms they now take. The Court has never known how to solve them, but it has had to deal with them in the past, in cases involving the creation of road-improvement and drainage districts and the like, in zoning cases, and in cases loosely and misleadingly characterized as concerning the delegation of governmental power to private groups.

Thus in *Browning* v. *Hooper,*[80] decided in 1926, a Texas statute authorized issuance of road-improvement bonds in any previously-established election district in a county, if two-thirds of the voters approved. The district was thus constituted a road-improvement district. The two-thirds majority that had voted the bonds in *Browning* v. *Hooper* came from one portion of the district, and most of the dissenting votes came from another. The dissenters, moreover, owned in the aggregate property of higher valuation than the two-thirds majority. The Court received the impression that what had happened was that

* See *supra,* pp. 65–69.

one large property owner had got together with many owners of property of little value in order to obtain an improvement that he wanted and that they were perhaps indifferent to, using the system to assess the cost of the improvement also on other, larger property owners who did not want it. This quite evidently struck the Court as unjust, and the remedy that suggested itself was enlargement of the constituency.

The legislature, said the Court, could create road-improvement districts, as had been held in some similar cases,[81] but the local voters could not—which is good Madisonian theory (the larger the constituency, the more factions, the less chance of majority tyranny), although a difficult general principle for judges to apply, if home rule and local government are to exist at all. In the alternative, the Court held, a judicial or quasi-judicial process must be interposed between the will of the majority and the individual's obligation to pay his share of the improvement, so that individual property owners can have a hearing on the question whether they would be benefited by the improvement. This remedy looks to individual justice, not to the problem of the proper constituency, and it is about equally called for, if at all, whatever the constituency may be. But, if the constituency is a proper one, may not the majority tax everyone for public purposes, those who will themselves be concretely benefited, and those who will not be? Moreover, the property owner who is in a numerical minority and who doesn't want to pay for an improvement even though it would benefit him is not going to be helped by a hearing. The real complaint of the dissenters in *Browning* v.

Hooper was that they wanted a constituency in which their power to affect political decisions would be greater.

In *Eubank* v. *Richmond*,[82] decided in 1912, two-thirds of the owners of property abutting a street were authorized to impose a building line, which would bind them as well as the minority. The Court held such a coercion of the minority to lack due process; but the opinion is cryptic, its reasoning mysterious. In a later case,[83] a similar arrangement was held bad on the ground that it constituted an improper delegation of governmental power to private groups, but in the meantime the Court had also, in another case, reached the contrary conclusion.[84] The conferral of power on professional and trade groups to govern themselves in one or another respect has been upheld or not with little rhyme or reason.[85]

A procedural remedy, such as the Court alternately proposed in *Browning* v. *Hooper,* is appropriate when the delegation is to a professional group which is given power to discipline individuals. On occasion, the alignment of interests may be such that the majority's interest runs counter to that of an individual member in quite striking fashion, more unmistakably than in *Browning* v. *Hooper,* as when chiropractors or faith healers are put under the governance of medical doctors, or producers of milk are subjected to regulation by consumers, or dealers by producers. To include a permanent minority in a constituency in which its natural enemy, so to speak, forms an equally permanent majority—having regard to the subject matter that is to be regulated—is rather hard, and no procedural device will appreciably soften the blow. In such a case, enlargement of the constituency is more clearly

155

indicated than in *Browning* v. *Hooper*. The majority in a larger constituency may wind up decreeing the same substantive result disfavoring the same minority interest, but there is a better chance that it won't, or that it won't always. At any rate, these are the exceptional cases, the relatively soluble ones. Elsewhere, any answer to the conundrum of proper constituency formation is highly elusive.

The delegation analysis is not helpful. It is useful when irresponsible power is exercised by administrative elites, and the Court demands that they be more closely controlled by a responsible elected body.[86] In the cases just discussed, power is, on the contrary, exercised democratically enough by the people concerned. The objection is not that the majoritarian principle has been disregarded, but that the majority has been allowed to abuse the rights of a minority. The problem, therefore, is not one of delegation, but of constituency formation. Enlarging the constituency, as by requiring the statewide legislature to act—the same result as when a delegation is held to have been improper; hence the confusion—is a natural answer. It is the answer suggested by Madisonian theory, and it commended itself to the Warren Court, as we have seen,* for reasons of its own. It appealed to the Court's sense of symmetry. In exceptional cases, as we have just noted, it is the proper answer. But although consistent both with abstract majoritarianism and with an aspect of Madisonian theory, it is far from producing the most democracy.

* See *supra*, pp. 112–115.

The larger the constituency, the less of a sense of participation can the individual voter have. The desire for participatory democracy, for more power on the part of people immediately concerned to affect decisions that rule their lives, will be met, not by the enlargement of constituencies, but by their contraction. Moreover, if a constituency is formed, as in the zoning or road-improvement or trade and professional association cases, or in political subdivisions, for the purpose of governing its members on one or on all subjects, then enlargement of it even at a cost in immediacy of participation may give distinct minorities a better hold on power, and be fairer to them. But if the constituency is formed for the purpose of representing its members in a central governing body, then the larger the constituency, the less likely is a distinct minority to be represented. Indeed, no purpose is served by enlarging home-rule or other special governing constituencies unless there is some assurance that the minorities to be protected in this fashion will find representation in the governing body of the larger constituency.

The structuring of government in terms of clearly defined interests, as when power is directly conferred on private groups to govern themselves, causes unease. It raises the specter of the corporate state, or of the medieval state, which classified people by status, and held them to the status in which they were classified. The individual is less free to withdraw from a constituency defined in professional or other status terms than from a geographic one, and our law values the freedom of the individual to dissociate himself even from the total national constituency; we recognize a right of expatriation.[87] And yet politics does deal with people's interests, and some interest-group autonomy is desirable.

There are things that matter very much to some people, and little if at all to others, and there are matters that some people know about intimately and others hardly at all. When the aversion to taking account of clearly defined interests is brought to bear on the formation of representative constituencies, moreover, it becomes merely symbolic, for even if interests (factions, as Madison called them) should not govern themselves, they should surely be heard—unless we could make them go away, which we cannot. We compromise, therefore, between our symbolic needs and a most exigent practical necessity by districting geographically. Yet a concentration of an appropriate group will not automatically coincide with a random geographical district, even though every act of districting will in some measure favor one or another group, however haphazardly. The compromise can be intelligent only if, through the formation of appropriate districts, people of like interests are enabled to concert together in politics.

Questions of constituency formation present themselves now and will continue to present themselves in many guises and in endless variety. There is the unadorned case—the most intractable, and least likely, perhaps, to induce judicial intervention—in which the claim is simply that equal districts could have been carved out in some other way than that adopted by the legislature, and that in choosing its way the legislature was motivated either by party considerations or by the desire to help incumbents retain office.[88] Then there are disputes about multimember districts. Legislators from such districts, sharing the constituency within which they are all elected at large, will often fail to represent some interests that might have formed a smaller single-member district; there will be groups in the multi-member constituency that are virtually permanent minorities. The majority, moreover, enjoys disproportionate power through its several legislative representatives, as compared with what may be a numerically almost equal majority in a smaller district with fewer members.[89] But, so far, the Supreme Court has indicated no general disapproval of multi-member districting.[90]

Racial connotations make for a special case of both the conventional and multi-member districting problems. Even before it tackled other aspects of apportionment, the Supreme Court did not hesitate to forbid formation of a constituency for blatant, and blatantly malevolent, racial reasons. When Alabama decided to segregate the city of Tuskegee by excluding all Negro homes from the city limits, the Court put them back in.[91] What was done in Tuskegee was what the substantial property owners in *Browning* v. *Hooper* might have wanted to do, namely, create a homogeneous constituency of their own. The Supreme Court would not have said them nay, but excluding Negroes as such, and against their will, is a different matter.*

The Tuskegee case is the equivalent of the decisions striking down school-closing measures and tuition-grant statutes that were tied unmistakably to the intention to

* The Court also, incidentally, has forbidden mention of a candidate's race on the ballot. Anderson v. Martin, 375 U.S. 399 (1964).

maintain segregated public schools. At least as much unease is caused, moreover, by a politics openly and rigidly
structured to represent racial groups in the society as by
the representation of interest groups otherwise so defined
in terms. But here also the compromise between the
symbolic undesirability of structuring politics in this fashion and the reality that the society does consist of identifiable ethnic and racial groups is struck by geographic
districting; and the compromise is meaningless if the
geographic districts do not even approximately take account of the groups. The problem is greatly more difficult,
therefore, when the claim is not that a racial group has
been blatantly classified as such to its disadvantage, but
that district lines have been knowingly drawn, or districts
have been enlarged, with the consequence that the political strength of a group is increased or diluted. For the
question then is not whether this may be done at all, but
whether, viewing the districting scheme as a whole, it was
done unfairly.

Quite early in the development of apportionment doctrine, the Court heard a case from New York City, where
the claim was that Manhattan had been gerrymandered so
as to produce one district with an overwhelmingly Negro–
Puerto Rican population. Congressman Adam Clayton
Powell, who represented this district, intervened on the
side of the defendants. The Court did not disturb the
arrangement.[92] Litigation turning on similar claims of
racial gerrymanders continues in New York, but incon-
clusively.[93]

There is apparently a good bit of multi-member constituency construction going on in several Southern states,

which is all fair and square under the one-man, one-vote
equal-district rule, but which has the effect of dispersing
Negro voters, and diluting or rendering entirely nugatory
any political power they might wish to exercise. The
Supreme Court has so far evolved no remedy.[94] One
federal court in Alabama struck down an apportionment
for the lower house of that state's legislature on the
ground that a multi-member district, consolidating three
previous single-member ones, was structured in this fashion for the sole purpose of preventing the election of a
Negro member of the house. "If this Court ignores the
long history of racial discrimination in Alabama," the
court declared, "it will prove that justice is both blind and
deaf."[95] But the case is, so far, a rarity.[96]

That the Warren Court was aware of the problem was
plain, and it was evident also that it hoped to get some
administrative help in dealing with it from the Attorney
General, whose authority to supervise and suspend
changes in Southern election laws under the Voting
Rights Act of 1965 the Court enhanced. One of the cases
that the Court in effect remitted to the augmented jurisdiction of the Attorney General involved "a change from
district to at-large voting for county supervisors." The
Court said: "The right to vote can be affected by a dilution of voting power as well as by an absolute prohibition
on casting a ballot. Voters who are members of a racial
minority might well be in the majority in one district, but
in a decided minority in the county as a whole. This type
of change could therefore nullify their ability to elect the
candidate of their choice just as would prohibiting some
of them from voting."[97]

Another category of constituency-formation problems that is moving into litigation is closely reminiscent of the older road-district and delegation-to-private-groups cases. It involves using status criteria to restrict the constituency that may vote for certain specified purposes within a political subdivision which, as such, forms the total constituency for general purposes. In two cases decided in June, 1969, the Warren Court showed little sympathy for, and perhaps an imperfect initial understanding of, the special constituency, and its possibilities for serving the objective of a more participatory democracy. *Cipriano* v. *City of Houma*[98] was relatively easy. A Louisiana statute provided that a municipality could issue bonds to finance publicly-owned gas, water, or electric utility systems only upon approval by a "majority in number and amount" of its property taxpayers. The bonds were in no way a charge on the city's property tax revenue, and thus on the property taxpayers. The bonds were to be serviced rather, and retired, out of the operating income of the utilities. The Court held the limitation of the franchise to property taxpayers unconstitutional as a denial of equal protection "to those otherwise qualified voters who are excluded." The Court was willing to assume for purposes of argument that in some circumstances only persons "specially interested" in an election might be permitted to vote, but it could not see how in this case other residents, who equally required the services of the utility systems, and who equally paid bills at low or high prevailing rates, were any less specially, or at all differently, interested in the election than property taxpayers.

In *Kramer* v. *Union Free School District*,[99] which has

significant implications for school decentralization, and for the renewed emphasis on the school as an extension of the family, the Court's decision was much more dubious. This case challenged a statute under which something less than one-third of school districts in New York—chiefly rural and suburban ones—were organized. The statute provided that the school district be governed by vote of the community, and it defined the community as residents of the school district who were owners or lessees of real property, and parents or guardians of children attending public schools in the district, whether or not they owned or leased real property. Voters so qualified approved the school budget and levied property taxes to pay for teachers' salaries and other school expenses, and they elected from their number three to nine trustees, who acted as the board of education, hired and dismissed teachers, set educational policy, and generally managed the schools. Thus the school district was to be run, as a lower federal court said in upholding the arrangement, by those who had the primary interest in its management, either because they carried the local financial burden or because they were parents of schoolchildren.

The Supreme Court, however, found a violation of the Equal Protection Clause. The Court, as also in the *Cipriano* case, paid lip service to a possible power of the state in some (not, apparently, easily conceived) circumstances to limit the franchise to voters primarily interested or affected. But the Court did not "reach the issue of whether these particular elections are of the type in which the franchise may be so limited," because in any event the classification made by the New York law did not

163

separate out voters "primarily interested in school affairs" with "sufficient precision" to justify denying a voice to others.

There should be little if any objection to the Court's undertaking to determine "whether all those excluded are in fact substantially less interested or affected than those the statute includes." But the New York statute excluded boarders and lodgers without school-age children, tax-free parents without school-age children, and tax-free parents whose children went to private school. It defies comprehension how these excluded groups could be deemed not to be "in fact substantially less interested or affected," unless the Court was telling us, without quite saying so, that the law may recognize no gradation of interest in public education, because the schools serve above all else the general interest of the society at large, and may not be confided to the care of the discrete communities that support them, or which they immediately serve—an ominous notion so far as school decentralization is concerned, but not really unexpected, as we have noted, coming from the Warren Court.

There was a suggestion in a footnote toward the end of the Court's opinion that what was really—or perhaps additionally—wrong with the classification attempted by the New York law was that it failed to take account of an individual's subjective interest in public education, which may or may not correspond to the objective criteria of interest that the statute used. A nontaxpaying bachelor, such as the plaintiff in the *Kramer* case, may have an intense interest, while a taxpaying bachelor, entitled to vote, may have no interest at all. But this sort of fixation on a subjective state of mind makes hash of any and all classifications. The uninterested bachelor must nevertheless pay his taxes. He is simply any nonparticipating qualified voter—some 30 or even 40 percent in the average Presidential election. There are disfranchised illiterates who may be more interested in elections than non-voting qualified literate citizens, as Justice Stewart pointed out in dissent in *Kramer,* and many a resident of New Jersey—or California, for the matter of that—may be more interested in a New York City election than certain indifferent residents.

The point of this catalogue of pending constituency formation problems is not that their solutions must sap the doctrinal foundation of the Warren Court's apportionment decisions, any more than in dealing with school decentralization or tuition-payment plans the Court need depart from the minimal requirement of *Brown* v. *Board of Education* that there be no segregation enforced by law. In both instances all that is in the offing is substantial irrelevance for those major decisions. The Supreme Court may well take on the constituency formation issue in all its varieties, as it may attempt also to ameliorate *de facto* school segregation, and it may muddle through, if to no very good purpose. Principled solutions are not probable. Constituency formation, like *de facto* segregation, will bring forth, not the judicial process, properly so-called, but the managerial talents of the judges, who may come up with answers that are better or worse, more or less expedient, and more or less acceptable than the initial decisions of electorally responsible institutions. That is as may be. There are other developments, however, which do seriously threaten the very survival of the one-man, one-vote rule. These developments are more evident or the local than on the state level, in school districts, in home-rule cities and in counties, and that is where the Court has encountered them.

One should have thought that the smaller the government, the simpler its concerns, and the smaller its constituency, the more nearly does it approximate the ideal of a town meeting. And that ideal, in turn, must be the model from which the one-man, one-vote principle proceeds. From the Warren Court's point of view, therefore, the nearer a case got to the town-meeting model, the more sensible and realistic it was to insist on one man, one vote, and the more prompt and absolute would that insistence be. This is not at all the conclusion to which a Madisonian insight leads. The greatest danger of majority tyranny, Madison thought, was to be found in a small direct democracy, which illustrated most plainly the error of "theoretic politicians" who supposed that "by reducing mankind to a perfect equality in their political rights" they could ensure a stable politics that would produce generally beneficial results. That could never be, Madison wrote in the Tenth Federalist, because the body politic consists of factions, groups, and when factions coalesce into a majority, they may oppress everyone else, unless power is dispersed. The smaller the unit of government, the fewer are the factions, and the more likely is majority tyranny. But that is Madisonian theory. The Warren Court's view has been that of the theoretic politicians who seek to reduce "mankind to a perfect equality in their political rights," and the Court should have found its views most easily applicable to the smallest units of government. And yet it was not so.

In the first local-government cases that came to it, the Warren Court hesitated. It exempted a school board by arbitrarily labeling its functions administrative, although surely the office of a governor is at least as much so, and yet in *Gray* v. *Sanders*[100] the Court decreed that governors must be elected on a one-man, one-vote basis; and it tolerated a method of electing a city council which bears a striking resemblance to malapportionment—at-large elections of the entire council, with a requirement that candidates be residents of various unequal districts.[101] Finally, however, in *Avery* v. *Midland County, Texas*,[102] the Court, while inscrutably projecting some possible future qualifications, declared that "precisely the same kind of deprivation [of constitutional rights] occurs when members of a city council, school board, or county governing board are elected from districts of substantially unequal population" as when members of a legislature are so elected. And the Court applied the one-man, one-vote rule to a board of county commissioners. In doing so, it lost Mr. Justice Fortas, who accused it of adopting a simplistic approach.

The Court, said Justice Fortas, had failed to take into account "a complex of values and factors, and not merely the arithmetic simplicity of one equals one." It had failed to recognize that the interests of all citizens in an elected body are not necessarily the same, and that governing bodies might have only slight and remote impact on some of their constituents, as for example inhabitants of home-rule cities, and a vast and direct impact on others. It had neglected to consider that much effective power is exercised by single executives elected by the entire constituency; that the power of such executives countervails that of malapportioned bodies with whom they are teamed; and that mathematical apportionment may result in representing one interest only, for example that of city dwellers, while entirely depriving other interests of power and even of a voice in their government.

The irony of Justice Fortas' dissent is that at the same time the Justice professed continued allegiance to *Reynolds* v. *Sims*[103] and other cases dealing with legislative apportionment. Yet everything he said holds for the larger units of government to which *Reynolds* v. *Sims* and like cases are applicable. Major cities have home rule, just as Justice Fortas pointed out the city of Midland in Midland County does, and that is just as relevant a consideration in assessing the relationship of a state legislature to its various constituencies as it is in judging whom the Midland County Commissioners really govern. And governors and other statewide officials are elected by the entire state, and their power countervails that of legislatures, just as the power of county executives countervails that of the Midland County Commissioners.* But, as a

---

* The sum of the argument, of course, as Justice Fortas' points demonstrate, is that, whether applied to the formation of legislatures or any other multi-member governing bodies, the majoritarian fixation of the one-man, one-vote rule may result in the denial of access and power to small groups that have distinct interests, and in the underrepresentation of larger groups. The large groups *may* find fair representation through fair equal districting, although the Court has devised no method to ensure the fairness of districting. Small groups will often be too small to be assured representation through equal districting. They can be included in the legislative

practical matter, it is indeed in school-board and other local-government cases that the difficulties created by the one-man, one-vote rule are most acute; it is here, where the Court, in obedience to principle and the demands of consistency, has finally applied the rule, that conditions will strain it until it must give way. When it does give way here, can it hold out elsewhere?

There are two directions, as we have seen, in which the organization of primary and secondary education in this country may move, and either way, the one-man, one-vote rule will be an unacceptable impediment. The movement may be as indicated by the present constitutional law of public schools, toward the hoped-for dispersal of racial and socio-economic groups. This is unavoidably the path of greater centralized control of schools. The consequence need not be, and very probably would not be, the abolition right off of local school boards, but it must at least be regional consolidation of them, federalization of them, if you will, under a supervening authority exercising some functions in behalf of all. It seems improbable that community influence will be disregarded to the point of con-

---

process through unequal districting, called malapportionment. It is possible to deprecate the need to so include them only if it is assumed, as the Warren Court chose to assume, that legislative policy is really made in elections, in which all groups have an equal chance, guaranteed by the one-man, one-vote rule, to coalesce with other ones in the formation of governing majorities. But this assumption is hardly realistic. The groups of which the society is constituted take part in the day-to-day governmental process chiefly by being represented in legislative bodies—by securing access, and thus a share of power. These views are set forth in Chapter V, "Reapportionment and Liberal Myths," of my *Politics and the Warren Court* (1965).

verting everything to an appointive system. If elective school boards, local and central, are employed, then either the one-man, one-vote rule must be abandoned, or the consolidation is politically impossible, as well as otherwise indefensible.

Outlying school districts are not likely, and should not be asked, to allow themselves to be governed by a central authority constituted on a one-man, one-vote basis, in which a major population center might control affairs. They cannot realistically or fairly be asked to submit themselves to governance by the central city, any more than the central city can allow them to govern. In the one case concerning a school-board apportionment problem that the Supreme Court has heard,[104] in which it arbitrarily labeled the central board administrative, there had been a consolidation of a number of local boards, themselves elected. A five-man central county board was to be chosen by delegates from the local boards, each board being entitled to one delegate. The city of Grand Rapids, with a population of over 200,000, dominates the county. It was held to one delegate, the same as smaller districts, four of which were indeed very tiny. This is no exceptional situation,[105] and it must become quite common if efforts to ameliorate *de facto* segregation are undertaken through various kinds of mergers of core-city and suburban school systems—which is the only practicable way.

The other and perhaps more likely direction in which the structure of public education may change is toward decentralization. Passing the constituency formation problem, and assuming that the Court is satisfied with the definition of a community which will run a decentralized

school, and with the definition of the appropriate electorate within it, it may be found desirable, at least in
initial stages, to retain a central board for the exercise of
some limited supervisory functions. There is no reason
why decentralized community school districts should be
equal in population, and there are many reasons why in
many instances they will not be. It will, therefore, again
be politically impossible, and inconsistent with the objective of community control of schools, to constitute a
central board on a one-man, one-vote basis.

The Court may again try to sweep school boards under
the rug by labeling them administrative, although it was
at pains not to do so in the *Midland County* case. Or the
Court may start, and seek to encourage, a trend toward
appointive rather than elected school boards—which is
not the trend now in being. No such expedients will avoid
other local government problems, however. For many
reasons additional to the racial one, but including it, the
structure of urban government is widely viewed as obsolete. The short of it is that the cities have most of the
troubles, but least of the middle class, and hence the
smallest tax base, although in the daylight hours, at any
rate, they serve the middle class. Cities are thus too small
a jurisdiction. They are also in many respects too large to
operate effectively and responsively.

The answer is to put the whole metropolitan area, city
and suburbs, under one government, covering a county if
it is large enough, or encompassing several counties if
they are small, and at the same time to decentralize control of some functions.[106] Depending on demographic
conditions, the result of organizing the new government

171

on a one-man, one-vote basis must be either that the suburbs are a permanent minority governed by the central city, or that the middle class in the suburbs combined with what is left of it in the city will govern a permanent minority of blacks and the poor. Neither result is politically feasible or fair, and a certain wariness toward metropolitan government is, therefore, evident in the Negro community.

There is no excess of cynicism in a suspicious reaction to proposals for metropolitan or regional government on a one-man, one-vote basis which follow the rise to power in the core city of Negro political leadership and even occasionally of a mayor. The solution must be Madisonian not majoritarian. Barring recondite devices, such as weighted voting, that make more trouble than they cure, or disingenuous disguises such as residence requirements, the solution is malapportionment by whatever name it is called. Yet, against it the Warren Court, emulated by many lower courts, dug in its heels.[107]

Proportional representation is a possible remedy, to be sure, consistent with one man, one vote. But it has proved disastrous on all but the smallest of scales; it defeats stable parties, and stable government. There is a device, used in Connecticut towns, on Pennsylvania county boards and in the New York City Council, for ensuring minority-party representation. It is not consistent with the one-man, one-vote rule, but it may sufficiently befuddle the issue to pass muster.[108] What is done is to fill two or three places on a commission or council by allowing each voter to vote for only one or two candidates; or else each party is permitted to nominate no more than one or two.

The result in either event is that the minority party is guaranteed a seat. But the device, workable in the two-party framework, is too rudimentary to solve the problem of group representation.

At the close of the Warren era, the Supreme Court confronts, in Auden's words, "that last picture common to us all,/ Of problems like relatives standing/ Puzzled and jealous." It may be that the Court can wiggle past the difficulties that loom in public-education and apportionment cases. They are not mere political obstacles, manifestations of willful resistance to the Court's principles; what is in question is the achievement of ends that, given ineluctable realities, are as plausibly desirable as those the Court strives for, and that ought not to be excluded, at least not as experimental objectives. If my probe into a near-term future is not wildly off the mark, therefore, the upshot is that the Warren Court's noblest enterprise—school desegregation—and its most popular enterprise—reapportionment—not to speak of school-prayer cases and those concerning aid to parochial schools, are heading toward obsolescence, and in large measure abandonment. And, if this assessment has any validity, it must be read as a lesson.

The future may yet belong to the Warren Court. There is no possible assurance to the contrary. But if the future follows more nearly the scenario I have just reviewed, then we must consider first of all whether the predicament might not have been escaped by a more faithful adherence to the method of analytical reason, and a less confident reliance on the intuitive judicial capacity to identify the course of progress. Pragmatic skepticism is certainly an attitude of its Progressive realist progenitors that the gallant Warren Court emulated all too little. More careful analysis of the realities on which it was imposing its law, and an appreciation of historical truth, with all its uncertainties, in lieu of a recital of selected historical slogans, would long since have rendered the Warren Court wary of its one-man, one-vote simplicities. The Court might have been inclined to stop shortly after its initial venture into the field, and to be content with striking down obsolete apportionments, with requiring legislatures to act after each census, and with formulating otherwise only the rule that at least one institution of a state government, commonly the executive, must be purely majoritarian.

Even so, analysis and history cannot alone refute an aspiration to a groupless society, to a politics without faction, and a theoretic preference, as Madison said, for "reducing mankind to a perfect equality in their political rights"*—a preference sustained by a prophetic judgment that the United States is now, or will soon be, so nearly classless a society that Madison's analysis is dated. And neither analysis nor history can prove that the secular, assimilationist public school is an unworthy ideal, or one which we should not struggle to attain. The lesson is not that there has been a basic malfunction in the judicial process. Better analysis, better history, a greater measure of pragmatic skepticism would have produced more caution, and less speedy development of doctrine. But ulti-

* See *supra*, p. 166.

mate doctrine could very well have been no different. The principles the Court has adopted are not irrational, they are not unfit for judicial pronouncement; the Court did not pluck them out of thin air, they do connect with strands in the tradition of our society.

The lesson, rather, is that in dealing with problems of great magnitude and pervasive ramifications, problems with complex roots and unpredictably multiplying off-shoots—in dealing with such problems, the society is best allowed to develop its own strands out of its tradition; it moves forward most effectively, perhaps, in empirical fashion, deploying its full tradition, in all its contradictions, not merely one or another self-contained aspect of it, as it retreats and advances, shifts and responds in accordance with experience, and with pressures brought to bear by the political process. The only abiding thing, as Brandeis liked to say, is change, and in those broad realms of social policy where that is so, judicial supremacy, we must conclude, is not possible.

The judicial process is too principle-prone and principle-bound—it has to be, there is no other justification or explanation for the role it plays. It is also too remote from conditions, and deals, case by case, with too narrow a slice of reality. It is not accessible to all the varied interests that are in play in any decision of great consequence. It is, very properly, independent. It is passive. It has difficulty controlling the stages by which it approaches a problem. It rushes forward too fast, or it lags; its pace hardly ever seems just right. For all these reasons, it is, in a vast, complex, changeable society, a most unsuitable instrument for the formation of policy.

175

Nothing is more evident in the Supreme Court's past than that most of its prior major enterprises—the better part of Marshall's nationalizing decisions being always a splendid exception—have not worked out. And yet nothing is more easily induced by the Supreme Court's past than complacency about its future. Somehow the Court has always managed to survive its failures. It has endured; hence perhaps it always will.

We wish it to endure—the people, it may be, have wished it to endure—because, aside from its forays into broad social policy, the Court discharges a much narrower, but still reasoned and principled, law-making function. It makes law interstitially, with effects that may be far-reaching and widely felt, if they are at all, only in the aggregate, over time. Someone must do this, whether an administrative elite or a more independent judicial one. Elected legislatures cannot do it prospectively, and no one can do it abstractly, outside the context of a concrete controversy. It might be done by a politically more responsive elite, but in the cases which call for performance of this task, a line between the demands of individual justice and the elements of more general policy is often difficult to draw. Thus the policy issue in the sort of speech case discussed in Chapter 3* is very closely tied to the question of individual justice. The same is true in most criminal-procedure cases. As an independent, politically unresponsive institution, the Court is relied on to do justice, and so we also let it make law in narrow compass.

* See *supra*, pp. 77–81.

There is a body of opinion—and there has been, throughout our history—which holds that the Court can well apply obvious principles, plainly acceptable to a generality of the population, because they are plainly stated in the Constitution (*e.g.*, the right to vote shall not be denied on account of race), or because they are almost universally shared; but the Court should not manufacture principle. However, although the Constitution plainly contains a number of admonitions, it states very few plain principles; and few are universally accepted. Principles that may be thought to have wide, if not universal, acceptance may not have it tomorrow, when the freshly-coined, quite novel principle may, in turn, prove acceptable. The true distinction, therefore, relevant to the bulk of the Court's business, lies not so much between more and less acceptable principles as between principles of different orders of magnitude and complexity in the application. This distinction can be sensed, and can serve as a caution, but no one has succeeded in defining it, and hence it is not serviceable as a rule. Unable to cabin the Court's interventions by rule, we have been generally content with the exercise of authority not so cabined. We do not confine the judges, we caution them. That, after all, is the legacy of Felix Frankfurter's career.

The society also values the capacity of the judges to draw its attention to issues of the largest principle that may have gone unheeded in the welter of its pragmatic doings. *Brown* v. *Board of Education* and other education cases, as also the reapportionment decisions, fulfilled this role of the Court. Having highlighted an issue of principle, however, the Court proceeds with the attempt to make the society live up to its resolution of it, which is another sort of function altogether. But again, since we are unable to formulate a rule that will ensure performance of the one function while guarding against assumption of the other, we tolerate both.

These are all reasons why the Court has endured. Another, perhaps the deepest, is a widely-shared if inarticulate hope that Learned Hand was wrong when he said "that a society so riven that the spirit of moderation is gone, no court *can* save." A society "where that spirit flourishes," Judge Hand added in this deservedly famous passage, "no court *need* save."[109] Here, I believe, he might have said "can," for he was talking about social policy made by judges, and they cannot, as I have just suggested, make it well. But is there not a chance that the judges might recall a riven society to its senses?

If we should encounter, not malapportionment, not inequality and social injustice, but a coup, an attempt by an inflamed majority or by a powerful elite, broken loose from other restraints, to proscribe and outlaw one or another group, or to mount a fundamental assault against broadly-responsive government, might not this unique American institution just save us? Nothing in the Court's past gives promise that it would, certainly not its stewardship of the Reconstruction Amendments in the first three-quarters of a century following the Civil War, or its passivity in face of the relocation of Japanese Americans during World War II, and the misbegotten attempt in the *Dred Scott* case to put the riven society back together scarcely promises that the Court could save us. Nothing in its past holds out the promise, excepting only the very fact of that continuous, lengthening past.

Because we hope that in the direst need the Court perhaps *can* save us—or to put it more realistically, may show us that we are not as riven as we feared—we allow it continually to try to save us when it cannot, and when authoritarian salvation is not what we need. We can afford the Court, but only because we are free to, and do, reject salvation from it nearly as often as it is tendered, and we can still afford it, even though it has seldom pushed its patent medicines so far so fast, in a society itself going far fast.

Over the entire "thrilling tradition of Anglo-American law," the natural trend has been toward the transfer of policy-making authority on one subject after another from judges to legislatures. That has been the movement of the common law itself. That also, in the long view, has been the movement of American constitutional law. A vast domain of social and economic policy, state and federal, occupied by the Court under the banner of the Commerce, Contract, Due Process and Equal Protection Clauses of the Constitution, is now the province of legislatures. Some initial decisions, as under the Commerce Clause, may still be left to the judges, with power to revise or reverse expressly reserved, however, to Congress. Some areas are taken over entirely by Congress, or parceled out to state legislatures. And always the judges cannot, unaided by Congress, carry to completion even enterprises they undertake on their sole—and formally unchallenged—responsibility.

179

The Court's assertion of judicial supremacy, although time-honored, stemming from John Marshall, is itself only one selected strand in our tradition. Congress, Presidents, and the states also make the Constitution. Deliberately or implicitly they have decided many a constitutional issue, and even where a prior constitutional adjudication by the Supreme Court existed, Congress has not always accepted the claim to judicial supremacy as validly establishing a judicial monopoly.[110] It has often taken the role of partner.

The rhetoric of Congressional debate about the Court turns on affirmations of a judicial monopoly, entirely excluding Congress, on the one hand, and angry claims to an entirely equal partnership between Court and Congress, on the other, if not to Congressional supremacy. That was the rhetoric of the debate on Title II of the Omnibus Crime Control and Safe Streets Act of 1968, which seeks, misguidedly in my judgment, to revise the *Miranda* case and like decisions on criminal procedure.[111] Through the fog, a more ambivalent, but real and enduring, position has been maintained, even by Title II of the Crime Control Act. Congress has understood that judicial supremacy would be intolerable if, in pursuance of the constitutional oath they, like the judges, also take, legislators and executives did not sometimes challenge the constitutional determinations of the Court—bending, supplementing, and finally displacing them. But Congress has also generally understood that intemperate challenges, let alone total and unqualified ones, would hazard the independence as well as denying the supremacy of the judges, and would remove a bulwark, or at any rate a symbol, that might just preserve and protect the very regime itself at some awful moment of supreme peril.

The true secret of the Court's survival is not, certainly, that in the universe of change it has been possessed of more permanent truth than other institutions, but rather that its authority, although asserted in absolute terms, is in practice limited and ambivalent, and with respect to any given enterprise or field of policy, temporary. In this accommodation, the Court endures. But only in this accommodation. For, by right, the idea of progress is common property.

Notes

1. The Warren Court

1. 347 U.S. 483 (1954).
2. Missouri ex rel. Gaines v. Canada, 305 U.S. 337 (1938); Sipuel v. Board of Regents, 332 U.S. 621 (1948); Sweatt v. Painter, 339 U.S. 629 (1950); McLaurin v. Oklahoma State Regents, 339 U.S. 637 (1950).
3. Terry v. Adams, 345 U.S. 461 (1953).
4. Shelley v. Kraemer, 334 U.S. 1 (1948); Barrows v. Jackson, 346 U.S. 249 (1953).
5. Youngstown Sheet and Tube Co. v. Sawyer, 343 U.S. 579 (1952).
6. See, *e.g.*, Garner v. Board of Public Works, 341 U.S. 716 (1951); Adler v. Board of Education, 342 U.S. 485 (1952); Knauff v. Shaughnessy, 338 U.S. 537 (1950); Carlson v. Landon, 342 U.S. 524 (1952); Harisiades v. Shaughnessy, 342 U.S. 580 (1952); Shaughnessy v. United States ex rel. Mezei, 345 U.S. 206 (1953).
7. 341 U.S. 494 (1951).

8. See, *e.g.*, Fisher v. Pace, 336 U.S. 155 (1949); Rogers v. United States, 340 U.S. 367 (1951); Sacher v. United States, 343 U.S. 1 (1952); Smith v. Baldi, 344 U.S. 561 (1953); Stein v. New York, 346 U.S. 156 (1953). See also Brinegar v. United States, 338 U.S. 160 (1949); United States v. Rabinowitz, 339 U.S. 56 (1950); On Lee v. United States, 343 U.S. 747 (1952).

9. Rosenberg v. United States, 346 U.S. 273 (1953).

10. Brown v. Board of Education, 349 U.S. 294 (1955).

11. 21 *U.S. Law Week*, 3164 (1952).

12. 22 *U.S. Law Week*, 3158, 3161 (1953).

13. Engel v. Vitale, 370 U.S. 421 (1962); School District of Abington v. Schempp, 374 U.S. 203 (1963).

14. Baker v. Carr, 369 U.S. 186 (1962); Wesberry v. Sanders, 376 U.S. 1 (1964); Reynolds v. Sims, 377 U.S. 533 (1964); Lucas v. Forty-fourth General Assembly, 377 U.S. 713 (1964); Avery v. Midland County, 390 U.S. 474 (1968).

15. See, *e.g.*, Gideon v. Wainwright, 372 U.S. 335 (1963); Brady v. Maryland, 373 U.S. 83 (1963); Malloy v. Hogan, 378 U.S. 1 (1964); Murphy v. Waterfront Commission, 378 U.S. 52 (1964); Sheppard v. Maxwell, 384 U.S. 333 (1966); Anders v. California, 386 U.S. 738 (1967); Mempa v. Rhay, 389 U.S. 128 (1967); Duncan v. Louisiana, 391 U.S. 145 (1968); Bloom v. Illinois, 391 U.S. 194 (1968); In re Gault, 387 U.S. 1 (1967).

16. Berger v. New York, 388 U.S. 41 (1967); Katz v. United States, 389 U.S. 347 (1967); Mapp v. Ohio, 367 U.S. 643 (1961); Lee v. Florida, 392 U.S. 378 (1968).

17. Miranda v. Arizona, 384 U.S. 436 (1966); United States v. Wade, 388 U.S. 218 (1967); Gilbert v. California, 388 U.S. 263 (1967); Mathis v. United States, 391 U.S. 1 (1968); Orozco v. Texas, 394 U.S. 324 (1969).

18. Flast v. Cohen, 392 U.S. 83 (1968).

19. See, *e.g.*, Evans v. Newton, 382 U.S. 296 (1966); United States v. Guest, 383 U.S. 745 (1966); Katzenbach v. Morgan, 384 U.S. 641 (1966); Reitman v. Mulkey, 387 U.S. 369 (1967).

20. Roth v. United States, 354 U.S. 476 (1957); Redrup v. New York, 386 U.S. 767 (1967).

21. Griswold v. Connecticut, 381 U.S. 479 (1965).

22. Aptheker v. Secretary of State, 378 U.S. 500 (1964); but cf. Zemel v. Rusk, 381 U.S. 1 (1965).

23. Schneider v. Rusk, 377 U.S. 163 (1964); Afroyim v. Rusk, 387 U.S. 253 (1967).

24. See, *e.g.*, Elfbrandt v. Russell, 384 U.S. 11 (1966); Keyishian v. Board of Regents, 385 U.S. 589 (1967); Whitehill v. Elkins, 389 U.S. 54 (1967); United States v. Robel, 389 U.S. 258 (1967).
25. See, *e.g.*, New York Times Co. v. Sullivan, 376 U.S. 254 (1964); Time, Inc. v. Hill, 385 U.S. 374 (1967); Curtis Publishing Co. v. Butts, 388 U.S. 130 (1967); Beckley Newspaper Corp. v. Hanks, 389 U.S. 81 (1967); St. Amant v. Thompson, 390 U.S. 727 (1968).
26. 82 Stat. 197 (1968).

2. The Heavenly City of the Twentieth-Century Justices

1. L. B. Namier, *Conflicts*, 70 (1942); and see E. H. Carr, *What Is History?*, 162 *et seq.* (1962).
2. Gray v. Sanders, 372 U.S. 368, 381 (1963).
3. See P. B. Kurland, "Foreword: 'Equal in Origin and Equal in Title to the Legislative and Executive Branches of the Government,'" 78 *Harvard Law Review*, 143 (1964).
4. Quoted in J. F. Paschal, *Mr. Justice Sutherland—A Man against the State*, 8 (1951).
5. D. J. Brewer, in *Dinner Given by the Bar of the Supreme Court of the United States to Mr. Justice John Marshall Harlan in Recognition of the Completion of Twenty-five Years of Distinguished Service on the Bench*, December 9, 1902, pp. 33, 34–36.
6. Quoted in R. H. Gabriel, *The Course of American Democratic Thought*, 402 (1940).
7. See R. Hofstadter, *Social Darwinism in American Thought* (rev. ed., 1955).
8. See Hearings Pursuant to Senate Res. 98, Committee on Interstate Commerce, 62nd Cong., 2d Sess., pp. 702–703 (1911–12).
9. Alexis de Tocqueville, *Democracy in America*, 137 (J. P. Mayer and M. Lerner, eds., 1966).
10. C. F. Amidon to Willis Van Devanter, Sept. 7, 1914, Van Devanter Papers, Library of Congress.
11. Wilson v. New, 243 U.S. 332 (1917).

12. Brandeis-Frankfurter Conversations, Brandeis Papers, Harvard Law School.
13. F. E. Warren to Willis Van Devanter, December 13, 1910, Van Devanter Papers, Library of Congress.
14. C. L. Becker, *The Heavenly City of the Eighteenth-Century Philosophers,* 7 (1932).
15. James R. Garfield to Charles Evans Hughes, April 27, 1910, Hughes Papers, Box 3A, Library of Congress.
16. 40 *American Bar Association Reports,* 365, 372 (1915).
17. F. Frankfurter, *Law and Politics,* 3, 6 (A. MacLeish and E. F. Prichard, Jr., eds., 1939).
18. 32 *Columbia Law Review,* 920, 921 (1932).
19. Brandeis Papers, Harvard Law School; W. H. Taft Papers, Library of Congress. The case in question was United States v. Moreland, 258 U.S. 433 (1922).
20. See, *e.g.,* T. R. Powell, "The Validity of State Legislation under the Webb-Kenyon Law," 2 *Southern Law Quarterly,* 112, 138–39 (1917).
21. T. R. Powell, "The Logic and Rhetoric of Constitutional Law," 15 *Journal of Philosophy, Psychology and Scientific Method,* 645, 646 (1918).
22. *Democracy in America, supra* n. 9, at p. 137.
23. *The Heavenly City of the Eighteenth-Century Philosophers, supra* n. 14, at p. 102.
24. 198 U.S. 45 (1905).
25. O. W. Holmes to Felix Frankfurter, Sept. 9, 1923, Holmes Papers, Harvard Law School.
26. Quoted in M. J. Pusey, *Charles Evans Hughes,* Vol. I, p. 287 (1957). See also Y. Rogat, "The Judge as Spectator," 31 *University of Chicago Law Review,* 213 (1964).
27. "Supreme Court, United States," 14 *Encyclopedia of Social Science,* 474, 480 (1934).
28. See L. Hand, *The Bill of Rights* (1958).
29. 262 U.S. 390 (1923).
30. 262 U.S. 404 (1923).
31. 268 U.S. 510 (1925).
32. *Law and Politics, supra* n. 17, at pp. 195, 196, 197.
33. *Ibid.,* n. 17.
34. Brandeis-Frankfurter Conversations, Brandeis Papers, Harvard Law School. See Whitney v. California, 274 U.S. 357, 372, 373 (1927).
35. Debs v. United States, 249 U.S. 211 (1919).
36. Schenck v. United States, 249 U.S. 47 (1919).

37. 252 U.S. 239 (1920).
38. 251 U.S. 466 (1920).
39. Brandeis-Frankfurter Conversations, Brandeis Papers, Harvard Law School.
40. See F. Frankfurter, *Of Law and Men*, 20 (P. Elman, ed., 1956); see *e.g.*, Pennsylvania Coal Company v. Mahon, 260 U.S. 393 (1922); Wolff Packing Co. v. Court of Industrial Relations, 262 U.S. 522 (1923); Thompson v. Consolidated Gas Utilities Corp., 300 U.S. 55 (1937).
41. O. W. Holmes to Felix Frankfurter, April 20, 1921, Holmes Papers, Harvard Law School.
42. L. L. Jaffe, "Was Brandeis an Activist?" 80 *Harvard Law Review*, 986 (1967).
43. 277 U.S. 438 (1928), overruled by Katz v. United States, 389 U.S. 347 (1967).
44. 274 U.S. 357 (1927).
45. Dennis v. United States, 341 U.S. 494, 517, 525, 555–56 (1951).
46. 4 Wheat. 316 (1819); see J. B. Thayer, "The Origin and Scope of the American Doctrine of Constitutional Law," in *Legal Essays*, 1 (1908).
47. Pp. 4, 94.
48. Pp. 4, 127.
49. 346 U.S. 273, 301 (1953).
50. *Law and Politics, supra* n. 17, at p. 193.
51. 287 U.S. 45 (1932).
52. F. Frankfurter, "The Supreme Court Writes a Chapter on Man's Rights," in *Law and Politics, supra* n. 17, at pp. 189, 192.
53. See, *e.g.*, Harris v. United States, 331 U.S. 145 (1947) (dissenting); Rochin v. California, 342 U.S. 165 (1952); Irvine v. California, 347 U.S. 128 (1954) (dissenting). But cf. Wolf v. Colorado, 338 U.S. 25 (1949), and Frank v. Maryland, 359 U.S. 360 (1959), both of which have been overruled: Mapp v. Ohio, 367 U.S. 643 (1961); Camara v. Municipal Court, 387 U.S. 523 (1967).
54. See Everson v. Board of Education, 330 U.S. 1 (1947) (dissenting, with Jackson, Rutledge and Burton, JJ.); Zorach v. Clauson, 343 U.S. 306 (1952) (dissenting); Illinois ex rel. Mc-Collum v. Board of Education, 333 U.S. 203 (1948) (concurring); cf. McGowan v. Maryland, 366 U.S. 420 (1961).
55. H. S. Thomas, *Felix Frankfurter—Scholar on the Bench*, 45–68 (1960).

56. Minersville School District v. Gobitis, 310 U.S. 586 (1940); West Virginia State Board v. Barnette, 319 U.S. 624 (1943) (dissenting).
57. 354 U.S. 234 (1957) (concurring).
58. 354 U.S. at 267.
59. *Id.*
60. Lucas v. Forty-fourth General Assembly, 377 U.S. 713 (1964).
61. *Of Law and Men, supra* n. 40, at p. 39.
62. Nominations of Abe Fortas and Homer Thornberry, Hearings Before the Committee on the Judiciary, United States Senate, 90th Cong., 2d Sess., pp. 105–106, 213 (1968).
63. Harper v. Virginia Board of Elections, 383 U.S. 663, 670, 677–78, n. 7 (1966).
64. R. Hofstadter, *The American Political Tradition,* 47 (Vintage ed., 1959).
65. 367 U.S. 497 (1961).
66. 381 U.S. 479, 484 (1965).

3. The Web of Subjectivity

1. 1 Cranch 137 (1803).
2. 377 U.S. 533 (1964).
3. 376 U.S. 1 (1964).
4. 9 Wheat. 1 (1824).
5. 2 Pet. 245 (1829).
6. 372 U.S. 368 (1963).
7. 385 U.S. 231 (1966).
8. Alexis de Tocqueville, *Democracy in America,* 137 (J. P. Mayer and M. Lerner, eds., 1966).
9. 234 U.S. 548 (1914); see *Felix Frankfurter Reminisces,* 298–99 (H. B. Phillips, ed., 1960).
10. Holmes Papers, Harvard Law School. O. W. Holmes to W. H. Moody, September 30, 1914, copy in possession of the author.
11. 243 U.S. 332 (1917).
12. 383 U.S. 301 (1966).
13. 384 U.S. 641 (1966).
14. See also United States v. Guest, 383 U.S. 745 (1966) (Clark, Black, Fortas, JJ., and Brennan, J., Warren, C. J., and Douglas, J., concurring) (*semble*).
15. See A. Cox, *The Warren Court,* 62–69 (1968).
16. 392 U.S. 409 (1968).

17. See G. Casper, "Jones v. Mayer: Clio, Bemused and Confused Muse," *The Supreme Court Review*, 89 (P. B. Kurland, ed., 1968).

18. 384 U.S. 436, 442 (1966). Cf. H. J. Friendly, "The Bill of Rights as a Code of Criminal Procedure," 53 *California Law Review*, 929, 944 (1965). For other judicial misadventures with history, see, *e.g.*, Wesberry v. Sanders, 376 U.S. 1 (1964); Afroyim v. Rusk, 387 U.S. 253 (1967).

19. See C. Peter Magrath, "The Obscenity Cases: Grapes of Roth," *The Supreme Court Review*, 7, 24 (P. B. Kurland, ed., 1966); H. Kalven, Jr., "The Metaphysics of the Law of Obscenity," *The Supreme Court Review*, 1, 43 (P. B. Kurland, ed., 1960).

20. Memoirs v. Massachusetts, 383 U.S. 413 (1966); Mishkin v. New York, 383 U.S. 502 (1966); Ginzburg v. United States, 383 U.S. 463 (1966).

21. See Magrath, "The Obscenity Cases: Grapes of Roth," *supra* n. 19.

22. Ginzburg v. United States, *supra* n. 20, at 468–69, n. 9.

23. Redrup v. New York, 386 U.S. 767 (1967).

24. Compare Naim v. Naim, 197 Va. 80, 87 S.E. 2d 749, *vacated*, 350 U.S. 891 (1955), *on remand*, 197 Va. 734, 90 S.E. 2d 849, *appeal dismissed*, 350 U.S. 985 (1956), with Loving v. Virginia, 388 U.S. 1 (1967), and H. Wechsler, "Toward Neutral Principles of Constitutional Law," 73 *Harvard Law Review*, 1, 34 (1959), with A. M. Bickel, *The Least Dangerous Branch*, 174 (1962).

25. 384 U.S. 436 (1966).

26. Compare Griffin v. Illinois, 351 U.S. 12 (1956), Jackson v. Denno, 378 U.S. 368 (1964), Roberts v. Russell, 392 U.S. 293 (1968), McConnell v. Rhay, 393 U.S. 2 (1968), Arsenault v. Massachusetts, 393 U.S. 5 (1968), and Berger v. California, 393 U.S. 314 (1969), with Linkletter v. Walker, 381 U.S. 618 (1965), and Tehan v. United States *ex rel.* Shott, 382 U.S. 406 (1966).

27. Johnson v. New Jersey, 384 U.S. 719 (1966); Stovall v. Denno, 388 U.S. 293 (1967); DeStefano v. Woods, 392 U.S. 631 (1968); Fuller v. Alaska, 393 U.S. 80 (1968); Desist v. United States, 394 U.S. 244 (1969); Kaiser v. New York, 394 U.S. 280 (1969); Halliday v. United States, 394 U.S. 831 (1969).

28. See, *e.g.*, cases beginning with No. 68, Turner v. Texas, 384 U.S. 1021–25 (1966).

29. Stovall v. Denno, *supra* n. 27, 388 U.S. at p. 301.

30. Linkletter v. Walker, *supra* n. 26, 381 U.S. at p. 622, n. 3.
31. See, *e.g.,* Gayle v. Browder, 352 U.S. 903 (1956); Holmes v. City of Atlanta, 350 U.S. 879 (1955); Mayor of Baltimore v. Dawson, 350 U.S. 877 (1955); Muir v. Louisville Park Theatrical Ass'n, 347 U.S. 971 (1954). Wilson v. Girard, 354 U.S. 524 (1957). See A. Sacks, "Foreword," 68 *Harvard Law Review,* 96, 99–103 (1954); E. J. Brown, "Foreword: Process of Law," 72 *Harvard Law Review,* 77 (1958).
32. South Carolina v. Katzenbach, 383 U.S. 301, 307 (1966); Georgia v. Pennsylvania R. R., 324 U.S. 439 (1945).
33. 383 U.S. 663 (1966).
34. Cox, *supra* n. 15, at pp. 125, 134.
35. L. Henkin, "Foreword: On Drawing Lines," 82 *Harvard Law Review,* 63 (1968).
36. Cf. Carrington v. Rash, 380 U.S. 89 (1965).
37. *Supra* n. 13.
38. See P. A. Freund, *On Understanding the Supreme Court,* 88, and see also 87–89 (1950).
39. See Morgan v. Katzenbach, 247 F. Supp. 196, 204 (D.D.C. 1965); and see United States v. County Board of Elections of Monroe County, 248 F. Supp. 316 (W.D.N.Y. 1965), *appeal dismissed for want of jurisdiction,* 383 U.S. 575 (1966).
40. 392 U.S. 83, 102–103 (1968).
41. See Frothingham v. Mellon, 262 U.S. 447 (1923).
42. Frothingham v. Mellon, *supra* n. 41.
43. See Henkin, *supra* n. 35, 82 *Harvard Law Review,* at pp. 72–76 (1968); but cf. Hearings before Subcommittee No. 3 of the Committee on the Judiciary, House of Representatives on H.R. 1198 and S. 3, 90th Cong., 2d Sess., pp. 131–42 (1968) (Testimony of Professor Paul A. Freund).
44. Horne v. Federal Reserve Bank, 344 F. 2d 725 (8th Cir., 1965); Protestants and Other Americans United for the Separation of Church and State v. O'Brien, 272 F. Supp. 712 (D.D.C. 1967), *reversed and remanded,* 407 F. 2d 1264 (D.C. Cir., 1968); see also Richardson v. Sokol, 285 F. Supp. 866 (W.D. Penna., 1968).
45. 387 U.S. 369 (1967).
46. Compare Smith v. Allwright, 321 U.S. 649 (1944); Terry v. Adams, 345 U.S. 461 (1953); Evans v. Newton, 382 U.S. 296 (1966).
47. C. L. Black, Jr., "Foreword: 'State Action,' Equal Protection, and California's Proposition 14," 81 *Harvard Law Review* 69, 82 (1967).

48. Cf. Gomillion v. Lightfoot, 364 U.S. 339 (1960); Guinn v. United States, 238 U.S. 347 (1915); Lane v. Wilson, 307 U.S. 268 (1939).
49. 393 U.S. 385 (1969).
50. *New York Constitution,* Article XI, Sec. 3; cf. Board of Education v. Allen, 392 U.S. 236 (1968).
51. Otey v. Common Council of City of Milwaukee, 281 F. Supp. 264 (E.D. Wisc. 1968).
52. Spaulding v. Blair, 403 F. 2d 862 (4th Cir., 1968).
53. Holland v. Lucas County Board of Elections, *cert. denied,* 393 U.S. 1080 (1969); see Petition for Writ of Certiorari, and Brief of Respondent in Opposition, Id., No. 77, October Term, 1968.
54. See, *e.g.,* United States v. O'Brien, 391 U.S. 367 (1968).
55. Cf. Holmes v. Leadbetter, 294 F. Supp. 991 (E.D. Mich. 1968); Ranjel v. City of Lansing, 293 F. Supp. 301 (W.D. Mich. 1969).
56. Griffin v. County School Board, 377 U.S. 218 (1964).
57. K. L. Karst and H. W. Horowitz, "Reitman v. Mulkey: A Telophase of Substantive Equal Protection," *The Supreme Court Review,* 39, 55 (P. B. Kurland, ed., 1967).
58. *Felix Frankfurter Reminisces, supra* n. 9.
59. See, *e.g.,* Maxwell v. Bishop, 398 F. 2d 138 (8th Cir., 1968), *cert. granted,* 393 U.S. 997 (1968), *reargument ordered,* 395 U.S. 918 (1969); Hill v. Nelson, 271 F. Supp. 439, 272 F. Supp. 790 (N.D. Calif., 1967); *New York Times,* Dec. 31, 1968, p. 17, col. 1 (" '68 Ending With No Executions, First Such Year in U.S. Records").
60. But cf. Rudolph v. Alabama, 375 U.S. 889 (1963); and see H. L. Packer, "Making the Punishment Fit the Crime," 77 *Harvard Law Review,* 1071 (1964).
61. Trop v. Dulles, 356 U.S. 86, 101 (1958).
62. Witherspoon v. Illinois, 391 U.S. 510, 519–21, 523, 541, 519–20, n. 15 (1968); and see Boulden v. Holman, 394 U.S. 478 (1969).
63. 390 U.S. 570 (1968).
64. See "The Supreme Court, 1967 Term," 82 *Harvard Law Review,* 95, 161–62 (1968).
65. P. A. Freund, *On Understanding the Supreme Court,* 27–28 (1951).
66. 308 U.S. 147, 161 (1939); see also Martin v. Struthers, 319 U.S. 141 (1943).
67. See, *e.g.,* NAACP v. Alabama, 357 U.S. 449 (1958); Bates v. Little Rock, 361 U.S. 516 (1960); Shelton v. Tucker, 364 U.S.

479 (1960) (*semble*); NAACP v. Button, 371 U.S. 415 (1963); Brown v. Louisiana, 383 U.S. 131 (1966) (*semble*); Amalgamated Food Employees Union Local 590 v. Logan Valley Plaza, Inc., 391 U.S. 308 (1968); but cf., Adderley v. Florida, 385 U.S. 39 (1966).

68. See, *e.g.*, Stromberg v. California, 283 U.S. 359 (1931); West Virginia State Board v. Barnette, 319 U.S. 624 (1943); Garner v. Louisiana, 368 U.S. 157, 196 (1961) (Harlan, J., concurring); Brown v. Louisiana, 383 U.S. 131 (1966); Thornhill v. Alabama, 310 U.S. 88 (1940); but cf. International Brotherhood of Teamsters v. Vogt, 354 U.S. 284 (1957).

69. 391 U.S. 367 (1968); see also United States v. Miller, 367 F. 2d 72 (2d Cir., 1966).

70. 36 *U.S. Law Week*, 3301, 3302–3306 (1968); cf. Street v. New York, 394 U.S. 576 (1969).

71. See R. A. Dahl, *A Preface to Democratic Theory*, 132 (1956).

72. See, *e.g.*, Lane v. Wilson, 307 U.S. 268 (1939); Smith v. Allwright, 321 U.S. 649 (1944).

73. See Hirabayashi v. United States, 320 U.S. 81 (1943); Korematsu v. United States, 323 U.S. 214 (1944); and see Ex parte Endo, 323 U.S. 283 (1944).

74. See Scales v. United States, 367 U.S. 203 (1961); Noto v. United States, 367 U.S. 290 (1961).

75. Beauharnais v. Illinois, 343 U.S. 250 (1952); but cf. New York Times Co. v. Sullivan, 376 U.S. 254 (1964).

76. See R. A. Dahl, "Decision-Making in a Democracy: The Supreme Court as a National Policy-Maker," 6 *Journal of Public Law*, 279 (1957).

77. See Nominations of Abe Fortas and Homer Thornberry, Hearings before the Committee on the Judiciary, United States Senate, 90th Cong., 2d Sess., pp. 181–222, 247 (1968).

78. Voting Rights Act of 1965, 79 Stat. 437 (1965).

79. See, *e.g.*, *New York Times*, March 26, 1969, p. 1, col. 3 ("Pennsylvanians Lead School Prayer Revolt").

80. 82 Stat. 197 (1968).

81. *Supra* n. 18.

82. 388 U.S. 218 (1967).

83. See J. G. Deutsch, "Neutrality, Legitimacy, and the Supreme Court: Some Intersections between Law and Political Science," 20 *Stanford Law Review*, 169 (1968).

84. *Supra* n. 20.

85. But cf. G. Gunther, "Reflections on *Robel:* It's Not What the Court Did But the Way That It Did It," 20 *Stanford Law Review*, 1140 (1968).

86. Jones v. Mayer Co., 392 U.S. 409, 444, 449, n. 6 (1968).
87. H. M. Hart, Jr., "Foreword: The Time Chart of the Justices," 73 *Harvard Law Review*, 84, 99 (1959).
88. See A. M. Bickel, *The Least Dangerous Branch* (1962).
89. Wechsler, *supra* n. 24, 73 *Harvard Law Review* at p. 27.
90. Wechsler, *supra* n. 24, 73 *Harvard Law Review* at p. 11.

4. Remembering the Future

1. See, *e.g.*, Griffin v. Illinois, 351 U.S. 12 (1956); Douglas v. California, 372 U.S. 353 (1963); Lane v. Brown, 372 U.S. 477 (1963); Draper v. Washington, 372 U.S. 487 (1963); see also Burns v. Ohio, 360 U.S. 252 (1959); Smith v. Bennett, 365 U.S. 708 (1961); Long v. Iowa, 385 U.S. 192 (1966); Roberts v. LaVallee, 389 U.S. 40 (1967).
2. See, *e.g.*, Ginzburg v. United States, 383 U.S. 463, 493 (1966) (Harlan, J., dissenting).
3. See Ker v. California, 374 U.S. 23 (1963); Aguilar v. Texas, 378 U.S. 108 (1964).
4. Columbus v. Mercantile Trust Co., 218 U.S. 645, 663 (1910).
5. 331 F. 2d 1000, 1004, 1017 (D.C. Cir., 1964), *cert. denied*, 377 U.S. 978 (1964); cf. Jehovah's Witnesses v. King County Hospital Unit No. 1, 278 F. Supp. 488 (W. D. Wash. 1967).
6. 239 F. Supp. 752 (D. Conn. 1965).
7. See, *e.g.*, International News Service v. Associated Press, 248 U.S. 215, 248 (1918) (Brandeis, J., dissenting); Truax v. Corrigan, 257 U.S. 312, 354 (1921) (Brandeis, J., dissenting); United Steelworkers of America v. Bouligny, Inc., 382 U.S. 145 (1965).
8. See Holmes v. United States, 391 U.S. 936 (1968); Hart v. United States, 391 U.S. 956 (1968); McArthur v. Clifford, 393 U.S. 1002 (1968).
9. See *supra*, p. 57, n. 29.
10. Reynolds v. Sims, 377 U.S. 533, 562, 565, 579–80 (1964).
11. Lucas v. Colorado General Assembly, 377 U.S. 713 (1964).
12. Kirkpatrick v. Preisler, 394 U.S. 526, 533 (1969).
13. Fortson v. Morris, 385 U.S. 231, 233, 249, 250 (1966).
14. Brandeis to Paul U. Kellogg, Nov. 7, 1920, Brandeis Papers, Law School of the University of Louisville; see A. M. Bickel, *The Unpublished Opinions of Mr. Justice Brandeis*, 119 *et. seq.* (1957).
15. See Colgrove v. Green, 328 U.S. 549, 556 (1946).

16. 21 *U.S. Law Week,* 3164 (1952).
17. *E.g.,* Johnson v. Virginia, 373 U.S. 61 (1963); Holmes v. City of Atlanta, 350 U.S. 879 (1955).
18. See H. Wechsler, *Principles, Politics and Fundamental Law,* xiv (1961).
19. See, *e.g.,* United States v. Jefferson County Board of Education, 372 F. 2d 836, 380 F. 2d 385 (5th Cir., 1966, 1967), *cert. denied, sub nom.* Caddo Parish School Board v. United States, 389 U.S. 840 (1967).
20. See, *e.g.,* Morean v. Board of Education, 42 N.J. 237, 200 A. 2d 97 (1964); Booker v. Board of Education, 45 N.J. 161, 212 A. 2d 1 (1965); Balaban v. Rubin, 14 N.Y. 2d 193, 199 N.E. 2d. 375, *cert. denied,* 379 U.S. 881 (1964); Vetere v. Allen, 15 N.Y. 2d 259, 206 N.E. 2d 174, *cert denied,* 382 U.S. 825 (1965); School Committee of Boston v. Board of Education, 352 Mass. 693, 227 N.E. 2d 729 (1967), *appeal dismissed,* 389 U.S. 572 (1968); Pennsylvania Human Relations Commission v. Chester School District, 427 Pa. 157, 233 A. 2d 290 (1967); Tometz v. Board of Education, 39 Ill. 2d 593, 237 N.E. 2d 498 (1968); Fuller v. Volk, 230 F. Supp. 25 (D.N.J., 1964), *vacated and remanded,* 351 F. 2d 323 (3rd Cir., 1965), *on remand,* 250 F. Supp. 81 (D.N.J., 1966); Offermann v. Nitkowski, 378 F. 2d 22 (2d Cir., 1967).
21. Brown v. Board of Education, 347 U.S. 483, 493–94 (1954).
22. See B. Bailyn, *Education in the Forming of American Society,* 15–49, (1960).
23. See M. DeW. Howe, *The Garden and the Wilderness,* 130–31 (1965).
24. R. A. Dahl, *"Who Governs?,"* 317–18 (1961).
25. See A. Mann, "A Historical Overview: The *Lumpenproletariat,* Education, and Compensatory Action," in *The Quality of Inequality: Urban and Suburban Schools,* 9, 16 *et seq.* (C. U. Daly, ed. 1968); C. Greer, "Immigrants, Negroes and Public Schools," *The Urban Review,* Vol. III, Jan., 1969, p. 9.
26. McCollum v. Board of Education, 333 U.S. 203, 216–17, 231 (1948).
27. School District of Abington v. Schempp, 374 U.S. 203, 241–42 (1963).
28. Pierce v. Society of Sisters, 268 U.S. 510, 534–35 (1925); and see Farrington v. Tokushige, 273 U.S. 284 (1927).
29. 330 U.S. 1 (1947).
30. Board of Education of Central School District No. 1 v. Allen, 392 U.S. 236, 244 (1968).

31. School District of Abington v. Schempp, *supra* n. 27, 374 U.S. at 242.
32. See, *e.g.*, Stell v. Savannah-Chatham County Board of Education, 318 F. 2d 425 (5th Cir., 1963); Hall v. West, 335 F. 2d 481 (5th Cir., 1964).
33. See, *e.g.*, Bush v. Orleans Parish School Board, 138 F. Supp. 337 (E.D. La. 1956), *affirmed*, 242 F. 2d 156 (5th Cir., 1957), *cert. denied*, 354 U.S. 921 (1957); Cooper v. Aaron, 358 U.S. 1 (1958); Goss v. Board of Education, 373 U.S. 683 (1963); Rogers v. Paul, 382 U.S. 198 (1965); Lee v. Macon County Board of Education, 267 F. Supp. 458 (M.D. Ala., 1967), *affirmed*, 389 U.S. 215 (1967); Alabama NAACP State Conference v. Wallace, 269 F. Supp. 346 (M.D. Ala., 1967), *affirmed, sub nom.* Wallace v. United States, 389 U.S. 215 (1967); United States v. Crenshaw County Unit of United Klans of America, 290 F. Supp. 181 (1968); North Carolina Teachers Ass'n v. Asheboro Board of Education, 393 F. 2d 736 (4th Cir., 1968); United States v. Board of Education of Bessemer, 396 F. 2d 44 (5th Cir., 1968).
34. Civil Rights Act of 1964, Titles IV and VI, 78 Stat. 246, 252 (1964).
35. James v. Almond, 170 F. Supp. 331 (E.D. Va., 1959), *appeal dismissed*, 359 U.S. 1006 (1959); Aaron v. McKinley, 173 F. Supp. 944 (E.D. Ark., 1959), *affirmed sub nom.*, Faubus v. Aaron, 361 U.S. 197 (1959); Griffin v. County School Board of Prince Edward County, 377 U.S. 218 (1964).
36. Griffin v. Board of Supervisors of Prince Edward County, 339 F. 2d 486 (4th Cir., 1964); Lee v. Macon County Board of Education, *supra*, n. 33.
37. See United States v. Jefferson County Board of Education, *supra* n. 19.
38. United States v. Montgomery County Board of Education, 395 U.S. 225 (1969).
39. Green v. County School Board of New Kent County, 391 U.S. 430, 439, 441 (1968). See also Raney v. Board of Education, 391 U.S. 443 (1968). And see Walker v. County School Board, 413 F. 2d 53 (4th Cir., 1969); Anthony v. Marshall County Board of Education, 409 F. 2d 1287 (5th Cir., 1969); Felder v. Harnett County Board of Education, 409 F. 2d 1070 (4th Cir., 1969); Davis v. Board of School Commissioners, 393 F. 2d 690 (5th Cir., 1968); Kelley v. Altheimer Public School District, 297 F. Supp. 753 (E.D. Ark., 1969); Acree v. County Board of Education, 294 F. Supp. 1034 (S.D. Ga.,

1968); Boomer v. Beaufort County Board of Education, 294 F. Supp. 179 (E.D. N.C., 1968); Moses v. Washington Parish School Board, 276 F. Supp. 834 (E.D. La., 1967).

40. Monroe v. Board of Commissioners, 391 U.S. 450, 457 (1968).

41. Board of Public Instruction of Duval County, Florida v. Braxton, 402 F. 2d 900 (5th Cir., 1968); and see Henry v. Clarksdale Municipal District, 409 F. 2d 682 (5th Cir., 1969); United States v. Greenwood Municipal District, 406 F. 2d 1086 (5th Cir., 1969); Swann v. Charlotte-Mecklenburg Board of Education, 300 F. Supp. 1358 (W.D. N.C., 1969).

42. See *e.g.*, Bivins v. Board of Public Education and Orphanage for Bibb County, Georgia, 284 F. Supp. 888 (M.D. Ga., 1967); Lee v. Macon County Board of Education, 289 F. Supp. 975 (M.D. Ala., 1968); Moore v. Tangipahoa Parish School Board, 298 F. Supp. 283 (E.D. La., 1968); but cf. Broussard v. Houston Independent School District, 395 F. 2d 817 (5th Cir., 1968); Griggs v. Cook, 384 F. 2d 705 (5th Cir., 1967).

43. See United States Commission on Civil Rights, *Racial Isolation in the Public Schools*, 1–59 (1967).

44. See Deal v. Cincinnati Board of Education, 369 F. 2d 55 (6th Cir., 1966), *cert. denied*, 389 U.S. 847 (1967); Downs v. Board of Education, 336 F. 2d 988 (10th Cir., 1964), *cert. denied*, 380 U.S. 914 (1965); Bell v. School City of Gary, Ind., 324 F. 2d 209 (7th Cir., 1963), *cert. denied*, 377 U.S. 924 (1964); Hobson v. Hansen, 269 F. Supp. 401 (D.D.C., 1967), *remanded*, Smuck v. Hobson, 408 F. 2d 175 (D.C. Cir., 1969); Springfield School Committee v. Barksdale, 348 F. 2d 261 (1st Cir., 1965); Blocker v. Board of Education, 226 F. Supp. 208, 229 F. Supp. 709, 714 (E.D. N.Y., 1964); Branche v. Board of Education, 204 F. Supp. 150 (E.D. N.Y., 1962).

45. See United States v. School District 151 of Cook County, Ill., 404 F. 2d 1125 (7th Cir., 1968), *on remand*, 301 F. Supp. 201 (N.D. Ill., 1969); Board of Education v. Dowell, 375 F. 2d 158 (10th cir., 1967), *cert. denied*, 387 U.S. 931 (1967); Taylor v. Board of Education, 294 F. 2d 36 (2d Cir., 1961), *cert. denied*, 368 U.S. 940 (1961), 221 F. Supp. 275 (S.D. N.Y., 1963); Clemons v. Board of Education, 228 F. 2d 853 (6th Cir., 1956), *cert. denied*, 350 U.S. 1006 (1956).

46. Compare Deal v. Cincinnati Board of Education, *supra* n. 44, and Downs v. Board of Education, *supra* n. 44, with Evans v. Buchanan, 207 F. Supp. 820 (D. Del., 1962).

47. See N. V. Sullivan, "Desegregation Techniques," in U.S. Commission on Civil Rights, *Racial Isolation in the Public Schools*, Vol. 2, p. 285 (1967). See, *e.g.*, cases cited *supra* n. 20.

48. See particularly Smuck v. Hobson, *supra* n. 44.

49. O. Fiss, "Racial Imbalance in the Public Schools, 78 *Harvard Law Review*, 564 (1965).

50. See Lee v. Macon County Board of Education, 267 F. Supp. 458 (M.D. Ala., 1967), *affirmed*, 389 U.S. 215 (1967).

51. See McInnis v. Shapiro, 293 F. Supp. 327 (N.D. Ill., 1968), *affirmed, sub nom.* McInnis v. Ogilvie, 394 U.S. 322 (1969); cf. Hargrave v. McKinney, 413 F. 2d 320 (5th Cir., 1969); Rodriguez v. San Antonio School District, 299 F. Supp. 476 (W.D. Tex., 1969); and see A. E. Wise, *Rich Schools, Poor Schools* (1968); Ashley *et al.*, *The Quality of Inequality: Urban and Suburban Public Schools* (C. U. Daly, ed., 1968).

52. See Carlsbad Union School District v. Rafferty, 300 F. Supp. 434 (S.D. Calif., 1969); Hergenreter v. Hayden, 295 F. Supp. 251 (D. Kan., 1968); Shepheard v. Godwin, 280 F. Supp. 869 (E.D. Va., 1968); Douglas Independent School District v. Jorgenson, 293 F. Supp. 849 (D.C. S.D. 1968).

53. Monroe v. Board of Commissioners, *supra* n. 40, 391 U.S. at 459.

54. See J. S. Coleman *et al.*, *Equality of Educational Opportunity* (1966).

55. See, *e.g.*, C. V. Hamilton, "Race and Education: A Search for Legitimacy," 38 *Harvard Educational Review*, 669 (1968).

56. Compare Coleman, *supra* n. 54, with S. Bowles and H. M. Levin, "The Determinants of Scholastic Achievement," 3 *The Journal of Human Resources*, No. 1 (1968).

57. G. K. Gardner, "Liberty, the State and the School," 20 *Law and Contemporary Problems*, 184, 189, 191 (1955).

58. Act of April 27, 1969, Ch. 330, *McKinney's Session Law News of New York*, 425 (1969); see Board of Education of the City of New York, *Proposed Community School District System Plan* (1968).

59. Gardner, *supra* n. 57, at p. 192.

60. See M. Friedman, *Capitalism and Freedom*, 85–107 (1962); cf. C. Jencks, "Is the Public School Obsolete?" *The Public Interest*, Winter, 1966, pp. 18–27.

61. See T. Sizer and P. Whitten, "A Proposal for a Poor Children's Bill of Rights," *Psychology*, September, 1968, p. 59.

62. See Norwalk CORE v. Norwalk Board of Education, 298 F. Supp. 213 (D. Conn., 1969); Coppedge v. Franklin County Board of Education, 394 F. 2d 410, 413 (4th Cir., 1968); and see *New York Times*, Oct. 13, 1969, p. 52, col. 2 ("South's Negroes Fight for Good Schools").

63. See, *e.g.*, R. E. Morgan, *The Politics of Religious Conflict*, 39–40 (1968).

64. Griffin v. State Board of Education, 239 F. Supp. 560, 563 (E.D. Va., 1965).

65. 275 F. Supp. 833 (E.D. La., 1967).

66. Louisiana Financial Assistance Commission v. Poindexter, 389 U.S. 571 (1968); and see *Id.*, 296 F. Supp. 686 (E.D. La., 1968).

67. 197 F. Supp. 649 (E.D. La., 1961), *affirmed per cur.*, 368 U.S. 515 (1962).

68. See, *e.g.*, Salsburg v. Maryland, 346 U.S. 545 (1954); see McDonald v. Brewer, 205 F. Supp. 1135 (N.D. Ala., 1968).

69. See Palmer v. Thompson, 391 F. 2d 324 (5th Cir., 1967).

70. Hall v. St. Helena Parish, *supra* n. 67, 197 F. Supp. at p. 523.

71. Brown v. South Carolina State Board of Education, 296 F. Supp. 199 (D.S.C., 1968), *affirmed*, 393 U.S. 222 (1968).

72. Griffin v. State Board of Education, 296 F. Supp. 1178, 1181 (E.D. Va., 1969); see also Coffey v. State Educational Finance Commission, 296 F. Supp. 1389 (S.D. Miss., 1969).

73. See *supra* n. 62.

74. Cf. Sherbert v. Verner, 374 U.S. 398 (1963).

75. Cf. Stein v. Oshinsky, 348 F. 2d 999 (2d Cir., 1965).

76. *Supra* n. 21, 347 U.S. at 492–93.

77. Reynolds v. Sims, *supra* n. 10, 377 U.S. at 577.

78. See *e.g.*, Swann v. Adams, 385 U.S. 440 (1967); Kirkpatrick v. Preisler, *supra* n. 12; R. G. Dixon, Jr., *Democratic Representation*, 439–55 (1968).

79. See P. C. Neal, "Baker v. Carr: Politics in Search of Law," *The Supreme Court Review*, 252, and especially 276–77, 281 (P. B. Kurland, ed., 1962); J. D. Lucas, "Dragon in the Thicket: A Perusal of Gomillion v. Lightfoot, *The Supreme Court Review*, 194 (P. B. Kurland, ed., 1961).

80. 269 U.S. 396 (1926).

81. See Valley Farms Co. v. Westchester County, 261 U.S. 155 (1923); Cole v. Norborne Drainage District, 270 U.S. 45 (1926).

82. 226 U.S. 137 (1912).

83. Seattle Trust Co. v. Roberge, 278 U.S. 116 (1928).

84. Cusack Co. v. Chicago, 242 U.S. 526 (1917).
85. See Carter v. Carter Coal Co., 298 U.S. 238 (1936); United States v. Rock Royal Co-op, Inc., 307 U.S. 533 (1939); Old Dearborn Co. v. Seagram Corp., 299 U.S. 183 (1936); L. L. Jaffe, "Law Making by Private Groups," 51 *Harvard Law Review*, 201 (1937).
86. See, *e.g.*, Schechter Poultry Corp. v. United States, 295 U.S. 495 (1935); Kent v. Dulles, 357 U.S. 116 (1958).
87. See 15 Stat. 223 (1868).
88. See, *e.g.*, Wells v. Rockefeller, 394 U.S. 542 (1969).
89. See J. F. Banzhaf III, "Multi-Member Electoral Districts—Do They Violate the 'One Man, One Vote' Principle?" 75 *Yale Law Journal*, 1309 (1966).
90. See, *e.g.*, Swann v. Adams, 385 U.S. 440 (1967); Fortson v. Dorsey, 379 U.S. 433 (1965); Burns v. Richardson, 384 U.S. 73 (1966). But see Kruidenier v. McCulloch, 258 Iowa 1121, 142 N.W. 2d 355 (1966), *cert. denied*, 385 U.S. 851 (1966).
91. Gomillion v. Lightfoot, 364 U.S. 339 (1960).
92. Wright v. Rockefeller, 376 U.S. 52 (1964).
93. Cooper v. Power, 260 F. Supp. 207 (E.D. N.Y., 1966); Ince v. Rockefeller, 290 F. Supp. 878 (S.D. N.Y., 1968).
94. See *e.g.*, Mann v. Davis, 245 F. Supp. 241 (E.D. Va., 1965), *affirmed sub nom.* Burnette v. Davis, 382 U.S. 42 (1965); Kilgarlin v. Martin, 252 F. Supp. 404 (S.D. Tex., 1966), *reversed on other grounds sub nom.* Kilgarlin v. Hill, 386 U.S. 120 (1967).
95. Sims v. Baggett, 247 F. Supp. 96, 109 (M.D. Ala., 1965).
96. Compare Smith v. Paris, 257 F. Supp. 901 (M.D. Ala., 1966); Ellis v. Mayor and City Council of Baltimore, 267 F. Supp. 263 (D. Md., 1967).
97. Allen v. State Board of Elections, 393 U.S. 544, 569 (1969); cf. Perkins v. Matthews, 301 F. Supp. 565 (S.D. Miss., 1969).
98. Cipriano v. City of Houma, 395 U.S. 701 (1969); see also Pierce v. Village of Ossining, 292 F. Supp. 113 (S.D. N.Y., 1968).
99. 395 U.S. 621 (1969), *reversing*, 282 F. Supp. 70 (E.D. N.Y., 1968).
100. 372 U.S. 368 (1963).
101. Sailors v. Board of Education, 387 U.S. 105 (1967); Dusch v. Davis, 387 U.S. 112 (1967); see also, *e.g.*, Goldblatt v. City of Dallas, 279 F. Supp. 106 (N.D. Tex., 1968); Robertson v. Gallion, 282 F. Supp. 157 (M.D. Ala., 1968).

102. 390 U.S. 474, 480, 496 (1968).
103. *Supra* n. 10.
104. Sailors v. Board of Education, *supra* n. 101.
105. See, *e.g.*, Delozier v. Tyrone Area School Board, 247 F. Supp. 30 (W.D. Penn., 1965); Strickland v. Burns, 256 F. Supp. 824 (M.D. Tenn., 1966).
106. See, *e.g.*, Avery v. Midland County, *supra* n. 102, 390 U.S. at 486, 492–94 (Harlan, J. dissenting).
107. See also Hyden v. Baker, 286 F. Supp. 475 (M.D. Tenn., 1968); Taylor v. Monroe County Board of Supervisors, 394 F. 2d 333 (5th Cir., 1968).
108. See Dixon, *supra* n. 78, at pp. 521–22; Blaikie v. Wagner, 258 F. Supp. 364 (S.D. N.Y., 1965); see also Blaikie v. Power, 243 N.Y.S. 2d 185, 193 N.E. 2d 55 (1963), *appeal dismissed for the want of a substantial federal question*, 375 U.S. 439 (1964).
109. L. Hand, "The Contribution of an Independent Judiciary to Civilization," in *The Spirit of Liberty*, 181 (I. Dilliard, ed., 1952).
110. See D. G. Morgan, *Congress and the Constitution* (1966).
111. 82 Stat. 210 (1968); see, *e.g.*, 114 Cong. Rec., 90th Cong. 2d Sess., pp. 4750–54 (1968) (Senator McClellan); Id., p. 4853 (Senator Morse); Id. p. 4923 (Senator Tydings); Id., p. 5217 (Senator Ervin).

Index